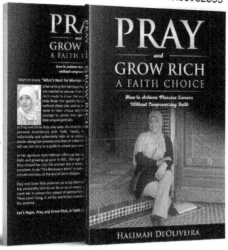

Pray & Grow Rich A Faith Choice

HOW TO ACHIEVE MASSIVE SUCCESS WITHOUT COMPROMISING FAITH

By Halimah DeOliveira

First edition published
March 2021
All production design are trademarks of Halimah Deoliveira

For information regarding bulk purchases of this book, digital
purchase and special discounts, please contact the author at

www.halimahdeoliveira.com

For Upcoming Stageplay cities
Email hello@halimahdeoliveira.com

"In the name of God, most Gracious, most Compassionate"

This book was written only by the permission of Allah ﷻ. Allah I thank you for your grace and patience as I grow into who You created me to be and allowing me to share my story and what I've learned along the way. I'm prayerful that it will be of benefit to the reader. This book is dedicated to every single person who has supported me in my business these last 4 years in a big or small way, I am appreciative all the same. To every kind hearted soul in Morocco who helped me along the way, those who helped me find my way through the airport, to the taxi drivers who made sure we reached our destinations and our guides both name Muhammad you opened me up to a whole new world and way of thinking. To Sonia thank you for saving space and allowing me to grow. To Gillian thank you for cheering me on! To Amber thank you for listening on the days when I thought I would fall apart, I made it!! Alhamdulillah. May God continue teaching and refining ALL OF US. Ameen

Authors Note

To the Women who are unsure of where they are going but know that there is more to life than the current way they are living. I wrote this book for you because I was once unsure, too. Within these pages is the story of how I was able to navigate my own journey, how God and consistent prayer have helped me and many women just like you both past and present get through.

Your life can be and look different if you want it to, if you're willing to put in the necessary work to achieve the life you desire.

I'm passionate about helping women just like you grow and make a positive impact in the life of your family and global community.

I'm sure you ask "Why am I so invested in you and I don't know you?" A Win for You is a Win for All of Us. We are One Ummah (one nation), we are like one body and we are only as strong as the weakest link.

I had plans to write this book 2 years ago and Impostor Syndrome set in, life got in the way and I was busy working on other projects but 2020 was the year that woke us all up and gave me the motivation I needed to write and release this book, now. If you have picked up this book years down the line 2020 was a year we will all remember as the year God held up a mirror and allowed us to come face to face with ourselves, the whole world all at once.

He pulled back the layers that busying ourselves created, He helped us see some ugly truths individually and collectively and then gave us the opportunity to do something about it. Many people lost their lives, livelihood, homes and life as they knew it in 2020. As I held empowerment programs online and spoke to women all across the world they were all saying the same thing, they were lacking that connection to God, that foundational support to help them to navigate these tough times. I knew the idea that had been rattling in my head for the last two years was the answer they needed. Not only did they need to be presented with the idea of faith as a solution to their problems in a practical way but they needed tools and resources to help them overcome their financial hardships. It's hard to get a woman to think about helping people outside of herself when her immediate needs, providing food and shelter for her children are not met. I felt I needed to give her that outlet so we lessen the chance of her ending up in a predicament like her current one in the future.

When I looked for books on Faith and Wealth there were a few things lacking, no Books written in layman's terms or that were relatable. There was little to no representation of women who looked like me. This book is my contribution to a path forward for us as Black. Muslim. Covered. Disenfranchised. Women.

If any or all of those titles resonate with you, read on. While we have created some of the negative situations we find ourselves in, there are others we have not. No matter which category you're in, IT IS YOUR RESPONSIBILITY TO MAKE YOUR WAY OUT! To be completely honest and transparent with you no one would blame us if we did nothing and conceded defeat or took the stance that some of the ills of the world are bigger than us, but then we become part of the problem and not the solution. Our ancestors planted seeds, we are still reaping the benefits and a harvest from today we have a responsibility to do the same for future generations, as women of faith we have a responsibility to stand up against injustice and preserve a more dignified way of life for our future generations. Through Prayer and Entrepreneurship we can create the blueprint with which our current and future generations can build on.

In what is my Signature style of writing I will share my stories and life lessons and through my transparency and vulnerability in sharing I pray I can be a helper, a mirror, a guide of sorts on your journey. Through my past experiences you can connect it to different times in your own life where you felt fear, overwhelm, loss etc. and see the lessons and the wisdom in those times and utilize them as fuel to keep going, to create better.

During our time together we will cover what I believe to be The 9 Principles of Success, it is my prayer that you read and dissect this book for the next 21 days and you refer back to it over time for inspiration and motivation. May it be a catalyst for change and lead to a total transformation of your life. The world needs your gift(s), your passion, your talents and most of all your love. Writing this book was extremely important to me because your success is important to me. Oftentimes we don't have access to people in our lives that genuinely are and take the time to listen to and care for us. Or that give us the opportunity to share our stories, offer a listening ear and prayerfully give us some advice and the right resources to manifest what we want in our lives

Upon completion of this book you will have a clearer understanding of where you are now, where you want to go and who you want to be in this world and the next.

In reading each of the Chapters of this book I pray you give rise to that small or even distant voice inside that wants to give birth to something greater. I am proof that no matter how destitute the life you are living now or off track you believe you are, it won't last always and with consistency and a few small shifts you can be in a totally different place tomorrow, 6 months and even 10 years from now. Allah(God) has promised us that He will take care of us, that He will not place burdens on us that are greater than what we can bear. Believe it. PRAY for what you TRULY WANT and don't settle or stop until you get it.

I'll see you on the inside.

Love,
Halimah

Table of Contents

1

Rock Bottom

Imagine if you will this scene where you and your dream husband are walking on the beach in your favorite country, mine happens to be Italy on the Amalfi coast, never been there but a girl can dream and inshallah it will happen one day. You've been married for a number of years, living a life you love and content with your life on all fronts faith, family, finances and your overall wellness. You think to yourself if I passed away today I would be content with everything God has blessed me with. Can I get a Mashallah?

From this same thought fast forward to the life you are living today and everything that you've gone through, it's hard to imagine this scene being a reality. What if I told you that this "Dream Life", that feeling of contentment is possible but you first have to grow through what you're going through now? Right here today whether you're in Rock Bottom or just come out of Rock Bottom, keep praying for what you seek. Impossibility and possibility are merely concepts of your mind, to Allah (God) nothing is impossible. He simply says *"Be" and it Is." Quran 36:82.*

Food Stamps & The Blue Coat

My Thoughts on Poverty

When I think of the life changing moments that formulated my initial "Money Story" it's the days we were on Public Assistance, standing in line waiting for cheese and canned goods and the Blue Coat Incident.

As the second oldest child and oldest girl one of my responsibilities as a kid was going to the store. I was around 8 when I first started going to the corner store on my own, an almost daily trip for an ingredient or two for that day's meal. Although I enjoyed the walk to the corner bodega in my hometown East New York, Brooklyn, I hated walking into the store and finding out it was crowded. That meant that whoever was in the store would see me pull out the Food Stamp Coupon booklet and show it to the clerk before I could remove the stamps and hand it to the clerk. As a kid I was grateful to have food to eat but didn't quite understand why we needed to be on public assistance and pulling out that booklet reminded me of my reality, that I was poor.

From age 8 through 12 we go through so many growing pains, coming into ourselves. The last thing you want is one more thing to have to worry about and to give someone something to say negative about you. As a result, I would always hang back and wait for everyone to leave, as did my older brother when we would go together. This way no one knew we were using food stamps. I remember hating this feeling, how people looked at you when you pulled out the coupon booklet to complete your purchase, dismissive and unapproving. Like somehow at 8 you were responsible for being in this predicament. Somehow I knew this limited our choices as to what we could ask for or afford. I vowed that when I got older I would have more control and say so over what foods or anything I could buy for that matter. I knew I wanted the power that money seemingly afforded other people.

On one of my solo trips to the Bodega, I had on my Teal winter coat, initially I loved this coat, it was knee length and puffy and had 4 pockets, two just above my waist so I could put my hands in to keep warm. And 2 lower pockets I could store my keys, money, gloves and the pack of 10 cent Now and Laters (a treat for being the one who went to the store) etc in. In addition to being my favorite coat, it was my only coat and would be for several years. My mom always bought a size or two up. I walked to the store and purchased eggs and the other items on the list. Some neighborhood kids came in the store as I was about to pay and I was mid attempt pulling out the food stamps from their perspective booklet to hand to the cashier, it was too late I couldn't hide this time. I paid and got my change and left the store.

As I was walking home the kids came out of the store and started following me, laughing at how I was using food stamps and making fun of my favorite coat. I wasn't so bothered by the food stamp or the coat comments but them following me didn't sit right with me as I didn't know their intentions and I needed to get back. I started walking faster to get away from them. The faster I walked, the faster they walked behind me. There were more of them than me so I held the grocery bag close to my chest and booked it the two New York City Blocks and the right turn onto my block and ran in my building. I wasn't going to wait and see what they had in mind. One block in I think they gave up chasing me but I kept running. Needless to say by the time I got to my building and up to my apartment on the second floor I had crushed the eggs and the yolk had seeped through the bag and was dripping down the front of my coat.

Initially my mother was upset, when she heard the story her anger subsided. I'll never forget that day because although I ran it taught me to stand up for myself. It also taught me years later the true value of money. That Teal coat my mom washed several times to try to get the egg smell out of it, I wore that coat for a few more years, that smell never came out of that coat, every now and then I would get a hint of the egg smell and I would be reminded of that day. It made me hate the coat even more, that smell reminded me of poverty and everything negative that resulted from it.

Now that I know more about the value of money I can extract more meaningful lessons from that story but at the time all I wanted was a new coat, so the smell wouldn't bring me back to that incident, but buying a new coat was not an option, we just didn't have the money to spare for a new coat for me. I remember vowing to purchase so many coats that I would never have to worry about only having one coat as an option. I knew in order to have what I thought was a more meaningful existence than the way I felt in my Blue Coat, at the local Bodega, with my food stamps, I needed to make lots of money when I grew up. I would grow up to do just that.

Poverty Mindset

Even at the age of 8, I understood the Power of Money, that it had the power to open doors that not having money couldn't. I was beginning to formulate my idea of money, my "Money Story", I didn't know it then but I had developed a "Poverty Mindset" I constantly worried about money and how often we didn't have it. So much so I worked to acquire it at every turn without any real direction for the money other than to possess it. Money without direction is easily spent and wasted. It's easier to make decisions based on fear, this is dangerous as it keeps you in victim mode, blaming others or putting responsibility on others to take care of you.

Like the first time I was presented with the idea of Investments in Real Estate, Business etc. I couldn't wrap my mind around giving up my money to invest in something that would give me a bigger return on my investment. Yet would waste $1000 or more on a new bag, wardrobe or pair of shoes. One produced wealth and the other gave the appearance of wealth. This Poverty Mindset does not just show up in the area of your finances it shows up in every area of your life. What you think is possible for you will be for you, just as what you don't think is possible for you will not be for you. The choice is yours.

The Cost of Love Without Focus and Faith

My wanting to escape the poverty that had plagued me my entire childhood led me to go into my first relationship. It's important to understand that the conversation around Faith and Finances are not far removed. The presence and the lack thereof of faith in the money conversation will lead to a girl or woman making decisions to acquire it out of want but in most cases necessity especially once she starts having children but I'm skipping ahead.

My first relationship started in my last year of high school, I just knew I was in Love y'all but honestly looking back I had connected with someone who had paid attention to me, listened to me in a way no one had before. I wanted out of the current life I was living, it was contradictory to what my life goals at the time were. I was taught not so much by conversation but by watching the adult role models in my life, go to school, get married and have children. So that's what I did.

At 20 years old I was in a four year relationship, with no real direction and I was expecting my first child. While I wasn't living in poverty I was not in the best financial situation to bring a child into, I also had no connection to faith, no true focus or direction in my life and definitely no financial direction or education.

No sooner than when my son was born I was separated and raising my son completely on my own. Bringing him into the world changed my perspective on things and I became more focused. I charted my career path and what I wanted, my boss at the time took the time to educate me on the true value of money. That not only could it change my life but it had the power to change the lives of the people around me (I wasn't ready to embrace the helping community part just yet).

The Business of Love

By this time I was moving up in my corporate job pretty quickly, I had gone from making $19k a year to $60k a year and had a pretty nice 401K savings and portfolio and was beginning to understand Real Estate and tap into my Entrepreneurial Bag.

I met my now Ex- Husband who had his own business and was on the rise. With a strong desire to have a father figure for my son and companionship for myself, it didn't take us long to get married. I know you're wondering "Halimah where does the Prayer part come into the mix?" Soon come Sis, soon come. This relationship was thought out like a business transaction in the beginning. My goal was financial stability, to grow even more than what I had built on my own for my son and myself and for my son to have a strong role model. To date this was my longest relationship, I believe it was in part because I was receiving exactly what I went into the relationship for, stability. Love came over time. What I forgot to ask God for was a spouse that was "Equally Yoked' or that could grow together with me spiritually.

When I was younger I wasn't as focused on faith as I should have been, I was very Dunya (worldly) focused and God blessed me with a partner that had the qualities I asked for. The moment I changed, evolved and wanted to have more of a connection with God the relationship began to crumble but not before child #2 came into the world. I hear stories from so many women that the babies keep coming and it keeps them stuck in situations they don't want to be in for lack of financial support. I pray that sharing this part of my story helps you to evaluate your current situation and work to change it before any irreversible negative consequences happen.

I was changing right before his and my own eyes. I felt trapped, I felt like I had outgrown the relationship and my partner wasn't willing to grow with me or in the direction I wanted to go. We had never had conversations about faith. If you are reading this and you are of a different faith than your potential spouse I strongly suggest you have a real conversation with yourself and your partner. When I started on my journey with my ex-husband I knew deep down that faith was important to me but at the time I needed to solve the more pressing concern which was a more stable living environment for my son. I didn't think that far ahead, but time passes and it passes quickly. Before I knew it ten years had passed and I was bringing another child into the world. I stayed in this relationship almost another two years despite being extremely unhappy and also having thoughts of returning to a more intentional spiritual practice. This time money was not an issue, we had managed to amass a healthy savings during our time together. Faith was missing and I had to let the relationship go. I was able to start over comfortably with my children. I began to make bigger and more intentional prayers and decisions.

For the Love of Faith

Many of you know my Faith Story from my Sophomore book "Not Without My Hijab: 11 Steps to Reclaiming Your Faith, let's just say I came back to Faith with a new found fervor but one that was so focused on the Akhirah that I lost focus of living in this world. It was in this time that I learned the Yin and Yang, the beauty of being focused on both the Dunya and Akhirah and the benefit of both.

It was at this time of reclaiming faith that I wanted to have a partner that I could share and grow in faith with. That could help me teach my children more about Islam, praying that they would follow me into faith. I began to lean into prayer more and ask God to understand more about the beloved religion of my birth.

I married my ex-husband, Husband #2, 6 months after returning to faith. On the day I got married I knew our relationship was doomed to fail. We had the faith part but everything else was missing. Needless to say we were divorced within a year. I share these stories with you because we have all been there in our own way. We have been where we make a poor choice and from making that first poor decision we make another choice or decision to try to fix the first and before we know it we are nowhere where we want to be. I needed to take a pause and a real hard look at what I wanted in every area of my life. I also needed to believe that it was possible. I needed Spiritual and Financial direction. I learned that these 3 men possessed some of the characteristics of what would make a great husband and life partner but I hadn't been specific enough in my prayers. More on this in Chapter 9: Be a Rich Wife.

Shifting Gears- Just Start

Somebody out there is asking well how do I start or create a plan. I'll be honest, I woke up one day and had a real conversation with myself. That conversation involved me sitting with a piece of paper writing down everything I wanted and everything that I didn't like about my life at the moment. I had a conversation with my ex-husband and children about life the way it was, it was not working for me and had to change. Within a few months of that conversation we were divorced and I began building my business and restructuring my life to what I wanted for myself and my children.

Prayers became a huge part of my decision making. I didn't move without first consulting God from praying Tahajjud daily and Istikharah for hard or major decisions. I took marriage, intimate partner relationships off the table. I didn't want to be in another relationship until I had completely thought through what the goal and purpose of my next relationship would be and I had created a better foundation for myself. I also knew there were other things that I wanted to accomplish as well and decided to make that my main focus.

How to make the Mindset Shift? I began telling myself a different story, that everything God had taken me through was for me and not just some punishment, that was happening to me. Every life event was preparing me for how I would serve Him and His people. I started reading more about the history of Great Women in Islam and what they were able to accomplish for themselves, their families and their community. I resonated with many of their stories. The way they impacted the world is the way I wanted to impact the world. I wanted to use my education and experience to help women and girls like me have the ability to make better decisions with regards to education, choosing their spouse, where they live etc. The better decisions we make for ourselves the more whole we become, the better off our children, families and ultimately our society will be.

RISE UP

This journey has not been easy. I have kept my therapist busy over the years. I know I'm not alone in this type of story around faith, money, business etc. Each of us has some negative and positive stories about money and faith and the pursuit of both. My goal in writing this book is to help us to see that no matter the trauma and negativity that moves around these two topics our complete spiritual and financial freedom is dependent on our healing in these areas. It's time to unlearn the harmful programming received as children that stifle us, stifle how we love, how we grow, evolve and show up for ourselves and others.

As a visibly black Muslim woman who is center stage unapologetically talking about two topics, faith and finances (that can be controversial depending on the circles, depending on the audience) its not easy to get people to understand how improvements in these areas can be of benefit. I know that our forward progress both in this life and the next are dependent upon us having a better understanding of how they can positively help us. As is my mantra an obstacle is often a stepping stone, to get you to where you want and need to be. Join me in Pray and Grow Rich: A Faith Choice where I'll be showing you how women just like you and I can achieve massive success without compromising our faith.

To the woman that picks up this book I pray you do this daily:

I pray you let go of ideas, people and things that no longer serve you,

I pray that God makes the transition and level up easy,

I pray you dare to dream,

I pray you dare to do,

I pray you dare to show up for you,

I pray you dare to write down your goals for this life and the next

I pray you dare to execute EVERYDAY.

Ameen

Reminder: God wouldn't encourage you to pray for something if He didn't want to bless you with it! Lessons in hardship, your trials did not come to harm you or punish you; they are there to guide you to what you truly want and to refine you, make you better and ultimately create a more intimate connection to your creator.

Most of my hardships have taught me to have more patience, more patience with myself, with other people and to give myself time, everything doesn't have to happen now, everything in due time.

What have your setbacks and hardships taught you?

Know this for sure, you can come back from anything by the power and the might of The Creator of course. Without Him you and none of this are possible. Do you believe you have the power to grow rich, to create spiritual and financial wealth? First you have to rid yourself of the limiting beliefs that popped into your head as you read that last question. What beliefs as a "Woman of Faith" do you hold about getting rich, living abundantly and creating wealth? (I have an exercise available on my website, www.halimahdeoliveira.com under the Pray and Grow rich tab.) 2020 afforded us a unique opportunity to change the world as we know it. How many of us can see that and are taking advantage of this once in a lifetime opportunity? And how many of us are willing to do the work necessary to rise up individually and collectively?

To "Rise Up" we must acknowledge that we are in fact in a place that is undesirable and we want to rise up from. The desire to rise up from the ashes is not enough; you have to be an active participant in your own rescue. One of the best ways to do this is to "Be Silent", Silence is a place of great power, healing and connection to God! In Not Without My Hijab: 11 Steps to Reclaiming Your Faith I talked about the importance and symbolism of the cave in Mexico, climbing out of my dark, old life, way of thinking and walking into the light and taking hold of everything God had to offer. Throughout history in many stories of prophets and believers there were times where they needed to ground and center themselves and they left the company of people and retreated to caves.

One of my favorite stories is of the Prophet Muhammad (SAW) during his time in the cave on Mount Hira, near Mecca that the Prophet Muhammad (SAW) first received revelation. We learn so much from this story on how our connection to God is what fuels our life; How God uses seemingly ordinary, unassuming people to show people how great He is. He starts out entrusting us with something small and as we grow into what we've been given He increases our territory, realm of responsibility.

Heal the Past

Overcoming Trauma and Fear

I have spent the last 4 years healing, healing from my past trauma, understanding triggers and how they can cause setbacks. Learning how to cope with triggers and new situations as they arise. Using what I learn from past mistakes to build something greater. Over the years I have had ups and downs with finances. The beauty about building a business from the ground up is if you did it once you can do it again. This time I'm playing for keeps and have been more intentional with the foundation on which I've built my life and business. I'm much more God conscious in everything I do. If you are ready to heal and build, continue to read on.

Pray and Grow Rich Formula: Rock Bottom

Chapter Reflection and Exercise

Begin with the end in mind as Stephen Covey said in his book, "7 Habits of Highly Effective People" a must read if you are in a place of transition and looking for transformation.

Try this exercise: Write out what you want the end of your life to look like; Who is there? What have you accomplished? Leave nothing out. Once you've created this now work backwards. Every single decision you make daily should be with that final scene in mind. Say "No" to anything not moving you towards that end goal.

With regards to your finances, what are the lessons you can learn from the past stories, the defining moments that stick out to you?

What is your intention for becoming wealthy? Is it purely financial? Spiritual? A mixture of both?

2

Dispelling Money Myths

Congratulations we made it out of Rock Bottom! In some cases these will be the worst of your days. That's not to say that there won't be more hardships and bad days. But with this new mindset shift you are now equipped with the tools and experience to recognize your current situation for what it is , a lesson, a chart on the course steering us to the right path and in the direction we want to go. Now it's time to tackle the issue of money and our negative beliefs around it.

Getting women to see and approach topics involving money, finances, business and self worth differently from a more positive perspective is very important to me. It's important to me because I know once they do they will make more informed decisions. They will approach marriage, work and other areas of life with more intelligence (Sabiduria, Hikmah). They will be able to choose out of choice, not desperation. Desperation has us make choices that may be positive in the short term and terrible for us in the long term.

In Chapter 1, I told you the story of Husband #2 who I learned how not to mishandle my finances from. But Husband #1 was the total opposite it was with him that I built and grew my empire. I went into that relationship knowing what I wanted from a Dunya (wordly) perspective and that's what I received. I will be sharing some of what I learned about the importance of Money, Faith, Boundaries and relationships from both of these experiences. Going back to the first chapter, to the Duas (prayers) we make.

We have to be real intentional and specific with God down to the most finite details. Allah (God) will give us what we pray for, be specific and intentional and don't think that you are being picky. Who taught us that we had to diminish our hopes and dreams to receive what we desire anyway? More than likely someone who had given up on the idea of having everything that they desired. Stop it!!! Let's get off that!

History of Women's Right to Money

Before we begin debunking or dispelling Money Myths we need to go back in history and talk about women's rights with regards to finances. With the development of our "Modern Civilization" women were given surprisingly less rights than their male counterparts. Over the years it has been ingrained into our culture that women somehow deserve to earn less and be treated differently. The goal of this brief history lesson is to show that the same way these ideals around women and money were learned they can be unlearned. The more we focus on helping women to understand their value and right to acquire wealth the further along our society will be.

As the old axiom goes: "Give a man a fish and he eats for a day. Teach a man to fish and he eats for a lifetime." But teach a woman to fish, and everyone eats for a lifetime.

Contrary to popular belief and many religious or cultural norms Women have the right to pursue a life that is pleasing to them within Religious boundaries and this includes entrepreneurship and wealth.

Ensuring we always take the middle path and are God conscious in every decision and action.

O people, we created you from the same male and female, and rendered you distinct peoples and tribes that you may recognize one another. The best among you in the sight of GOD is the most righteous. GOD is Omniscient, Cognizant.

Quran 49:13

And for all there are degrees [of reward and punishment] for what they have done, and [it is] so that He may fully compensate them for their deeds, and they will not be wronged.

Quran 46:19

Although a little known fact men and women had equal financial rights at various points in history.

In Islamic History, with the advent of Islam in the 6th Century Prophet Muhammad (SAW) ensured both women and men were allowed to own property, inherit estates and initiate divorce.

Women in Islam specifically have the right to own property, to control their own money, to buy and sell, and to give gifts and charity. It is impermissible for anyone to take a woman's wealth without her consent. Islam gave women the formal rights to an inheritance. Women in Islam also have the right to an education; As seeking and acquiring knowledge is an obligation on all Muslims and people of faith male or female.

Muslim women have the right to accept or refuse marriage proposals and married women are completely free from the obligation of supporting and maintaining the family. Working married women are free to contribute to the household expenses, or not, as they see fit. Don't let anyone guilt you into thinking you have to contribute from your money. Women have the right to seek divorce if it becomes necessary.

With this knowledge it should give us a sense of confidence in what is possible for us and also shows us what to look for in Life Partnerships and relationships. With regards to what we think about money it shows us that God is not against us having it as long as we are using it in a manner that is pleasing to him. As women with this historic knowledge as our foundation we can begin to dispel the myths we've been led to believe over the last 100 or so years about money.

Did you know it is only in the last 83 years that we have made substantial changes to benefit women economically?

Below is a timeline of some such examples in women's rights history in the US dating from 1938; This list includes some of the rights Islam gave to women 1400 + years ago.

Timeline of Women's Financial Rights

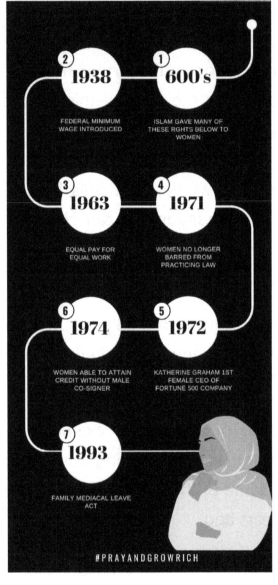

2 1938
FEDERAL MINIMUM WAGE INTRODUCED

1 600's
ISLAM GAVE MANY OF THESE RGHTS BELOW TO WOMEN

3 1963
EQUAL PAY FOR EQUAL WORK

4 1971
WOMEN NO LONGER BARRED FROM PRACTICING LAW

6 1974
WOMEN ABLE TO ATTAIN CREDIT WITHOUT MALE CO-SIGNER

5 1972
KATHERINE GRAHAM 1ST FEMALE CEO OF FORTUNE 500 COMPANY

7 1993
FAMILY MEDIACAL LEAVE ACT

#PRAYANDGROWRICH

I pray that trip down memory lane was helpful and opened you up to a world of possibility for yourself, your family and for posterity. Now let's dispel these myths so we can wipe the slate clean and begin to create and tell different stories both as women of faith, color and/or other disenfranchised groups.

The 5 Myths and The 5 Truths

Myth #1 "I Don't want to be rich or wealthy."

Truth#1

The first myth is one that I held onto for a long time, and this was " I don't want to be rich!" or "I'm terrible with money". Why do we repeat this phrase to ourselves? Why do we say it as if it's honorable? Why do we judge someone who desires more?

I hear phrases like this on a daily basis from women and particularly "Women of Faith" The desire to be poor or somehow being poor should be a badge of honor is something you learned or heard someone who wasn't rich or wealthy say and justify their reasoning with non-facts about the people that have it, they may even misquote scripture to justify it as well. It's something that was either passed down to them or because they hadn't mastered the skill to acquire wealth for themselves or had a skewed understanding of what being wealthy meant economically, religiously and even racially.

Our brain is wired to believe everything we tell it. The more we tell ourselves or others that that we don't want to be rich or I'm terrible with money, that's exactly what we will continue to believe and be. For years I believed I wasn't good with finances, as a single mother despite pay increases and a healthy salary at a young age I sabotaged myself at every turn and overspent for the sake of overspending. Despite making more money than both of my parents combined growing up at 21 and 22 years old I held on to their limiting beliefs and believed I didn't and wouldn't ever have enough.

Over the years every time I made a mistake, I got near the limit or maxed out a credit card, spent my whole paycheck on something frivolous and unnecessary, it was confirmed that I couldn't manage my money and therefore was NOT going to be rich or wealthy. But that I didn't desire it because it just wasn't attainable for me, I was in this repeated cycle where I beat myself up even more and ingrained the idea and belief even further into my subconscious and I continued this cycle until my Mid Twenties, Raise after Raise, Promotion after Promotion.

News flash, we ALL make mistakes, especially when it comes to money. Know that it's ok to make mistakes because we learn through our mistakes!!

Don't beat yourself up, through the lessons learned from these mistakes I'm writing a book with a chapter empowering women to change their limiting money beliefs so they can thrive in every area of their life, let that sink in.

It has taken me a long time to forgive myself over past mistakes in many areas of my life including my finances, I know it is what has held me back on many occasions.

What has gotten us as Women, Women of Faith and color to this point? Where we don't feel we are worthy of asking or wanting more. Shame, shame to admit that we don't know, that we are "Beginners' at something. Especially nowadays, everyone on Social Media is the Guru or Subject Matter Expert on something. We are ashamed to ask for help. That it somehow makes us smaller to need help with our finances. If this were true why are there financial advisors and consultants? Their role is to help you see your money as a tool and the bigger picture for what you're able to achieve with your money.

We have been taught to suppress our childlike curiosity and enthusiasm towards life and conform to the norm. I encourage you to be wild and free in your thoughts. Be courageous and curious, here's an example of what it may sound like "I don't know what this means, but I want to know." Try it out, say it aloud it is freeing to not know and ask questions. If I ask for help or pursue this inquiry I will know and then we will know. As women when we learn or acquire a skill it is in our nature to teach and nurture others. It is in this sharing that we learn, grow and evolve. Without the sharing of stories, asking questions, we won't see where we're going wrong and we'll never know the answer. Again we will be in this perpetual cycle of stagnance and unfulfillment.

Myth #2 Being Wealthy is Impious!

Truth #2

I have come across many women in my 20+ years working in both Corporate America and in business who believe because they are "Women of Faith" that somehow the attainment of wealth takes Heaven and the abundance of God's Blessings off the table. That somehow going through pain and staying broke or impoverished is going to earn them an additional reward that is better than that of a person who is affluent or wealthy.

I grew up in a very male dominated household where only men possessed money, wealth, they controlled how money was acquired and spent. It was contradictory to me watching my mother on welfare always making a dollar out of 15 cents while there was a male telling us that a man is the provider and that a woman is to honor and obey her husband. The woman who doesn't is impious. I was stuck between these two ideas that contradicted themselves and without my own understanding of faith, I took this as law and somehow saw this as the norm and desirable. I did not learn the true history of Islam and what Islam taught until I was much much older. It made sense why the males who yielded these made up religious concepts helped to keep the women in their lives in subservient almost captive positions. Fearing that they were being disobedient not only to their husbands but also going against their faith and God by wanting more for themselves or their families.

I was also taught that only evil people possessed money. So I like many of you subconsciously learned to cut off my access to it and make enough to live and managed a modest savings as a cushion.

Here is where you more than likely heard that it was better to be poor than rich and ran with it.

Abu Hurayrah narrated that the Prophet (SAW) said, "The poor will enter Paradise before the rich by half a day, and that is five hundred years." A day in the sight of Allah is like a thousand years, thus half a day is equivalent to five hundred years.

While this is true and we pray that we are of the people of the highest paradise, Jannatul Firdaus, there are other ways to gain a high status. Both Poverty and Wealth are Fitnah, tests of how we will comport ourselves with or without money. We have a responsibility in both.

In another hadith, he (SAW) stated,

> "Three things destroy, and three things save. As for the three things that destroy, they are: greediness that is obeyed, and desires that are followed, and a person becoming self-conceited (and proud) with himself. As for the three things that save, they are: the fear of Allah in secret and public, and moderation in poverty and richness, and fairness in anger and pleasure."

Who are you, we, to tell God who He should bless and who He shouldn't and how He should bless them. If He blessed you with wealth don't sabotage it and throw it away thinking that what you've been blessed with is somehow a mistake. What God has blessed you with is yours to carry out your duties as His servant with. If this statement were true what do we think of the many Sahabas and Sahabiyat who were wealthy and funded the advent of Islam? The first wife of the Prophet Muhamamd (SAW) was one of the most affluent women of her time, she is also one of the women who will enter paradise in spite of her wealth. Learning her story and her status helped me to reformulate my idea on money as a woman. We will cover more on this in the next chapter "The Women."

Whenever I was blessed with large sums of money I would find a way to sabotage it in some way. God stripping me of all my money was to teach me what it felt like to not have it so I could see its true value and purpose.

I finally learned how prayer works when I started my business four years ago. Everything I had earned prior to reclaiming faith I earned with great hardship and could only see the acquisition of it from my own capacity of output. If I work 16 hours I will earn this much money. When I started my business I stopped asking God for money and began asking for abundance and for Him to facilitate certain experiences for me. I began receiving endorsements, through collaborations with companies I received free products, vacations, trips etc in exchange for my speaking at an event. These additional perks came in addition to my income from my business, I now had money to contribute to charity. Perplexing how one small shift created all the opportunities I didn't have when I was actively pursuing them and thinking the lack of money was the issue. What was lacking was an abundant mindset.

When you understand the true meaning and value of money you understand that it becomes what you intend it to become. It will become Good if you start out earning it with good intentions and will become evil or bad if that's your focus.

Myth #3 Being Rich/ Wealthy Is an All or Nothing game!

Truth #3:

This is another myth that holds us back from the actual attainment of wealth. The I have it or don't attitude. So if my goal is to have $100,000 in savings we want to magically be able to go to the bank with the full $100,000 and deposit it. Instead of taking the attitude that I can begin with $100 and make small shifts in my budget, spending and increasing my earning potential and making those smaller deposits that will build up over time.

There's also the idea that I have to have more money or earn more money in order to begin to have the conversation about building wealth.

Wealth and abundance are a mindset before they're an asset. Meaning before we can have actual wealth we have to believe that it's possible. We also have to take care of our money when we have little. How does God know if He can trust you with more if you are not a good steward of the little money or blessings He gives you. Going back to the "Food Stamps & The Blue Coat" Story. The lesson I was supposed to catch was to be grateful for what I had. To develop an appreciation for having little so that when God blessed me with more that I knew who blessed me with it and what I was being entrusted to do with it.

So in going back to Being Rich is an all or nothing game, becoming wealthy is much like anything else as you learn and mature you will evolve and the goal is to increase in wealth both spiritually and financially.

Myth #4 I will be Wealthy Later

Truth #4 The Strategy that actually leads to Wealth

While there is no perfect blueprint for creating wealth there's only the strategy you create, and can consistently execute that will work for you.

This "I will be wealthy later" concept is the belief that wealth, abundance and riches are acquired or happen over time which can be true but not always the case. Many of you have this ideology, you believe that a part of being young is being free and not having to worry about responsibility including being good stewards of money. Halimah it's too early to think of the future, retirement, abundance or wealth. It's also the belief that somehow I can save my way to wealth, which FYI you cannot. You also cannot work your way to wealth. You can build up a healthy savings but it will not lead to wealth unless you put your money to work for you. This can be in the form of different types of investments. Be sure to check out the Boss

Hijabipreneur podcast for our many guests and episodes where we dive deeper into the different ways to create wealth.

Again it's as if wealth is something that happens for people later in life. The opportunity to attain wealth can come at any time from a number of different means. You could receive an inheritance, land a job that pays very well or make an in demand product or service and acquire wealth that way. Many businesses saw a surge in their in demand products or services in 2020. Although it was a challenging year many millionaires were made in 2020. If those entrepreneurs took the attitude that it is something that happens later they may have gotten in their own way and sabotaged it for themselves. We will discuss "5 Before 5" in a later chapter which basically talks about how we have to take care of 5 things before these other five things and one of them is our wealth before poverty.

When I was 22, a boss and mentor during my annual raise/review asked me "What I was doing about retirement?' I gave him a puzzled look, to which he responded " Thinking and planning for retirement isn't something you want to save for later. You want to begin having this conversation as early as possible as it will help you make more informed decisions with your finances along the way. It will help you to act with a sense of urgency and act on an opportunity immediately and not wait as it may be one of those once in a lifetime opportunities. The younger you are when you are presented with this ideology the better off you'll be in the long run. It will give you a headstart on thinking about money as it will serve you along the journey. So if you are a Mom, Aunt, Grandmother or Community leader of young girls share this chapter with her or them. The future is created in the now.

Myth #5 Budgeting Does Not Help Build Wealth

Truth #5

How will God know if He can trust you with greater wealth if you are squandering what you currently have? Being a Good Steward of your money is not just a catchy slogan it is how you will eventually grow your money.

Budgeting can in fact help you build wealth, learning to utilize your money better will help you to learn how to put your money to work for you. You can use your current job as a resource or tool to help you get out of debt and begin saving to invest. The difference between saving and investing is that saving allows you to put money away for a rainy day. Whereas saving to invest allows you to save money until a viable investment opportunity presents itself. One that will give you a return on your investment. Imagine multiplying money you have already saved.

A few ways you can Budget your money to later invest:

1- Saving On Car Payments or Other Monthly Bills (Don't Be Afraid to Shop Around)

2- Save on your Monthly Rent or Mortgage. Is there a way to improve your credit score and lower your monthly payment? Can you afford to downsize or move a community over where rent is cheaper? In some cases, temporarily paying down expenses living in a rental can save you on additional taxes and maintenance until you can truly afford to own a home.

3- Stop Buying Junk and things you don't really need; Develop a Minimalist Mindset if you don't absolutely "Love" the item Don't Buy it.

4- And of Course Save a Percentage of your Income remember

"Halimah's Golden Rule 50-30-10-10"

50% of your income goes to Housing and Expenses

30% of your income to Savings

10% of your income to Entertainment or Wants

10% of your income to Charity

5- Earn More Money

Counter Intuitive at first glance. Like Sis if I could earn more money so easily I wouldn't be in this situation. Change your mindset, when you make up your mind to do something it will happen Inshallah (God Willing) you just have to believe it will and put all your effort into it.

The younger you are the greater your chances of being successful; If you Work Hard when you're younger when you're older you won't have to work so hard to make your money work for you.

6- Invest in Your Education & Pursue Entrepreneurship

The more you know the better off you will be. Whether you go back to school to get a degree, take a certification course or learn via books, online courses, Google or Youtube never stop learning. When you stop learning you stop growing and before you know it you're back in that vicious cycle again repeating your parents mistakes or ones you made when you were younger.

One stream of income is not enough to sustain us. It can be gone in a blink of an eye. If our life giving sustenance is reliant on that income we should work to build up a cushion. We should also create a support system within our communities so we are not solely reliant and dependent on entities that may not have our best interests at heart.

7- Invest in Yourself and Your Marketing

For my fellow entrepreneurs whether you run your business full time or have a Part Time Hustle I will tell you in the 4 years since I started my business one thing I never regret is the time and money I spent investing in myself and my business. Whether it's Spiritual Development, Financial Development it all counts we can use them interchangeably in both our personal and professional life.

Marketing is another necessary investment whether you're an entrepreneur or employee. One of my Boss's/Mentors gave me the greatest advice: Dress for the Job or Position you want not the one you have, I never forgot that. I apply to my business, my marketing and to the way I help my clients market their businesses. If you make $1 million annually in your business but desire to make $3 million annually in your business what does your brand need to look, feel and sound like in order to attract that? The same goes if you are an employee and you want to earn a better salary, show up as the person that would earn that salary.

Myth #6 I have to be Hyper focused on Money to acquire wealth;

Truth #6 Stop Chasing Wealth and Become Abundant

I'll say it again, Wealth is a Mindset before it is an asset. How are you transforming your mindset to be one that attracts the wealth and abundance you desire vs chasing after a monetary sum with no real goal for your money once you do acquire it.

Wealth and Abundance do not only stem from money. Money is the direct result of intention and Consistency. Focus on Intentionally doing Good Deeds consistently and you will reap the benefits of your efforts.

While one of the focuses of this book is about financial wealth it isn't the only type of wealth. Before you can tackle having money you must first tackle having an abundant mindset. You must believe that Allah wants the best for you.

In the name of Allah, the Beneficent, the Merciful

Allah the Generous, in His infinite mercy, will multiply the good deeds of His righteous servants up to seven hundred times as much or even more.

Allah said:

مَّثَلُ الَّذِينَ يُنفِقُونَ أَمْوَالَهُمْ فِي سَبِيلِ اللَّهِ كَمَثَلِ حَبَّةٍ أَنبَتَتْ سَبْعَ سَنَابِلَ فِي كُلِّ سُنبُلَةٍ مِّائَةُ حَبَّةٍ ۗ وَاللَّهُ يُضَاعِفُ لِمَن يَشَاءُ ۚ وَاللَّهُ وَاسِعٌ عَلِيمٌ

The example of those who spend their wealth in the way of Allah is like a seed which grows seven spikes, in each spike is a hundred grains. Allah multiplies His reward for whom He wills, for Allah is vast and knowing.

Quran 2:261

Like a single seed from which springs forth hundreds of grains, Allah will cause the good deeds of His righteous servants to grow and multiply in a similar manner.

Abu Huraira reported: The Messenger of Allah, peace and blessings be upon him, said:

مَا تَصَدَّقَ أَحَدٌ بِصَدَقَةٍ مِنْ طَيِّبٍ وَلَا يَقْبَلُ اللَّهُ إِلَّا الطَّيِّبَ إِلَّا أَخَذَهَا الرَّحْمَنُ بِيَمِينِهِ وَإِنْ كَانَتْ تَمْرَةً فَتَرْبُو فِي كَفِّ الرَّحْمَنِ حَتَّى تَكُونَ أَعْظَمَ مِنْ الْجَبَلِ كَمَا يُرَبِّي أَحَدُكُمْ فَلُوَّهُ أَوْ فَصِيلَهُ

None gives charity from what is good, for Allah only accepts what is good, but that the Merciful takes it with His right hand. Even if it is a date, it is nurtured in the hand of the Merciful until it becomes greater than a mountain, just as one of you nurtures his young horse or camel.

Sahih Muslim 1014

57

Fix Your Attitude About Money

How many of these myths can you relate to? How many of these phrases have you uttered yourself? Let's turn these myths on their head and unlearn them.

The better idea is to want what Allah (God) has for you and to be content with what He wants to give you.

If He wants wealth for you, abundance for you. Don't Shoo it away. If He is blessing you with it, it is because He trusts you to do the right thing with it, to use it much like the Prophets (AS) and the Sahaba (RA) before you, in the way of bringing people closer to God, to experience their own enlightenment.

Take Care of Five Before Five

"Make the most of five things before five others: life before death, health before sickness, free time before becoming busy, youth before old age, and wealth before poverty."

A great idea to ponder over as you move forward through the later chapters. Each part of our lives, the people that come into and out of it play a role in the whole of who we are and how we impact the world and ourselves. Find the middle road in everything you do.

A person cannot remain upon two divergent paths, or retain a tight grip on two items moving in opposite directions. Given that the path to fulfilment of illicit worldly desires and the path to the pleasure of Allah travel in different directions, excessive love of wealth risks compromising obedience to Allah, and the blessings to be gained from seeking His pleasure. This section can be summarised in the hadith of the Prophet (SAW) in which he said,

"The plentiful (i.e., the rich) will be the lowest on the Day of Judgement, except he who distributed his money left and right (i.e., at all times), while he earned from pure (means)."

Pray and Grow Rich Formula: Dispel Your Own Money Myths

Chapter Reflection and Exercise

Observe where you think you've gone wrong in the past. Retrace your own history.

What are your limiting beliefs about money?

Where do you think these beliefs came from?

Write a list of all the times you've "messed up" with money, or where others have caused problems for you, like partners or family getting you into debt. Then, reframe the mistake or situation into something positive? What did you learn from it?

What is the New Money Story you want to tell?

What are some of the positives about having and earning more money?

What are some of the things you will do with your wealth?

3

The Women

The Power of Femininity

Do you know your true power? Women have the power to pull people, whole societies in towards truth. In looking back at 2020, and oppressed races and cultures, black people specifically were reminded of how enslaved we still are despite time moving forward. Here is a thought to ponder as the women of the society, we will not be liberated externally until we are liberated internally. People who adhere to faith are dangerous to societies whose main focus is on controlling the society with thoughts and ideals that keep them oppressed. People of faith know that man has no full control over them and that position is reserved for God. As women we are the preservers of culture, through our stories, Art, Music, education etc. we pass our history down to the next generation so that our culture, beliefs etc. continue.

Throughout history, societies have changed the true definition of femininity, the way God intended it by using a male ruler of measurement and so as women we constantly are coming from behind, trying to achieve some feat or assume roles we were not created to assume in hopes to get ahead. It is my goal to help you to see how truly powerful you are when you are being your authentic self. That we can take off the masks and release ourselves from the burden of responsibility of roles that we were never meant to assume and create a new standard. Learning to shed some of the thinking Society has worked to instill in us to keep us in a box that keeps us in many cases stuck.

What if I told you there was a time when the role of women in society was just as important if not more important than what it is today. If we look to history we will see that in periods of unrest it was the women that kept everyone grounded, the women that restored peace, tranquility and a sense of normalcy within the society. We are not only nurturers but we also bring a sense of reason and rationale to every situation. We think about the collective as opposed to the individual self.

Why is this important? In my global travels as a Business Strategist, I've met many women and one common theme they all have at some point in their life is they have felt unworthy and in some cases have been made to feel unworthy by a man or due to the influence of masculine ideals. My goal is to empower and to show that the masculine and feminine ideals are both necessary and that they were created to Co-exist equally, not one voice being more overpowering than the other. Having both provide balance and a balanced society is a successful society. Which is why when you see successful societies look to the status of the women in that society. Where the status of women was high the society flourished.

In this Chapter I invite you to meet 5 women from the past that we can each learn a lesson from to apply in every area of our life Faith, Family, Finances and Fitness (overall wellness) and a few women from the present, they are women I admire and who exemplify many of the characteristics of these amazing women from the past. What we can learn from these women is that the way God created us, our true essence stands the test of time, our values and what we want out of our time here on earth has not changed much although technology and societal norms may have changed. At our core we are still in pursuit of the same fundamental achievements and ideals as our ancestors. Through their stories I pray we can find a little bit of ourselves in them and utilize their failures, lessons learned and triumphs for forward progress in our own lives.

There was certainly in their stories a lesson for those of understanding. Never was the Qur'an a narration invented, but a confirmation of what was before it and a detailed explanation of all things and guidance and mercy for a people who believe.

(Quran 12:111)

Finding the Balance

No matter the faith tradition we often ask if a balance between motherhood, having a career and our many other roles, can ever be found. When we look to our faith we see how God clearly defines our roles as men and women and how everything circumvents those two main roles, we will achieve the balance. Without the balance faith offers we may feel like we have to choose one of these roles over another. What we learn from the 5 women we'll talk about in this chapter and many women throughout history is that they did not choose, they compartmentalized each of their roles.

Specifically in Islam, the role of a muslim woman is multi-faceted and endless. Allah ﷻ has given some responsibilities specifically to women, and others He has given to all of mankind; she is responsible for raising her children, being a good wife, of calling people to the beauty of Islam, of speaking out against oppression, of giving in charity, being kind to her neighbors, helping the poor, those in need – and so much more. We should take pride in these duties and responsibilities that Allah ﷻ has bestowed upon us and fulfill them to the best of our ability, by the standard He has set forth.

In studying the lives of the women we'll talk about in this chapter one thing they all understood was how short their time in the Dunya, worldly life was and so they acted with a sense of urgency with regards to seizing opportunities. There was a prescribed time to complete everything in their lives from prayer, to time with their children, friends & family, work etc. I'm sure they didn't have fancy planners like we do today but they ensured they scheduled and occupied their time with meaningful activities that helped them evolve and grow in some area. Pretty sure seven hours of endless Social Media scrolling was not on the agenda. I'm guilty, I've done it, so no judgement here.

Simultaneously understanding that their acts individually may have seemed insignificant but their collective actions made a great impact during their time and we reap the rewards until today.

They saw every opportunity put in front of them as significant and impactful no matter how small. What we can learn from this is even though society may tell us we can have it all, do it all, what we make our Kaaba or our priorities will dictate what we spend most of our time doing; the entirety of our lives will be defined by what we not only believe the purpose of this life is but also what we work towards. Allah ﷻ reminds us in the Quran:

"And I did not create the jinn and mankind except to worship Me."

Quran 51:56

From this ayat we can go back and reset our intentions, turn this ship around and make it go the right way.

The 5 Women Past and Present Lessons & Likenesses

What will we find when we examine the lives of these women more closely? I found that they enjoyed this life and used their time and everything they were blessed with to sustain them in this life in the pursuit of the next. So intelligent and profound how everything was used as an act of worship and in obedience to God.

Before we learn about these 5 women of the past and some of the women in the present that inspire me, I want to highlight one woman in particular that Allah, God sent into my life at the right time and for so many of the right reasons. Ameenah Muhammad-Diggins is an Award Winning Brand Strategist, Author, Speaker and Coach For Muslim and Believing Women.

I happened to meet Ameenah, at a woman's event in Philadelphia where she was the Mistress of Ceremonies. I loved her positive energy from the jump and when I went to talk to her after the event because I wanted to get to know more sisters doing amazing things in the community, I loved her instantly. I even asked her about a few masjids in the South Jersey area as I was travelling 45 minutes to an hour to attend Jummah (Friday Prayer for Muslims) every week. Turns out we lived close to each other in Jersey and she attended a mosque that was about 1-2 miles from my home and work. By far the best masjid I could have attended was Masjid GCLEA under the leadership of Imam John Starling and his wife Evana Cooper.

As a muslim woman returning to faith its often difficult to find a community that will embrace you as you are and give you the grace to grow in faith. That community and attending that masjid gave me the space I needed to grow. Everytime I think of my journey back to fully embracing Islam I remember Ameenah and I remember that Masjid that allowed me to grow into a better muslim and person. I not only admire her for her work but I owe her a debt of gratitude that I will never be able to repay. Ameenah Jazakallah Khair, may you reap the reward for every good deed that springs forth from our very first encounter. With that please read as Ameenah tells us the story of one of the great women of the quran, I pray you enjoy it and get as much out of it as I have.

Maryam, Mary RA

Something About Mary

Activating Faith and Gratitude

Written By: Ameenah Muhammad-Diggins

When Halimah asked me to write an excerpt for Pray and Grow Rich I knew that this was a project that was going to be an important addition to the self improvement books that I love. Then fear overtook me and as a result procrastination began. I had to take a look at myself and ask what was fueling my fear and subsequent procrastination. I was afraid that because I wasn't a scholar I was not qualified to write even one letter about the greatest women to have ever lived

To overcome this I asked Allah for guidance and for him to remove the fear. I then referenced the pious women who came before us for inspiration.

The task that I was given was to draw a parallel from their lives to ours. I thought about which of these illustrious women most resonated with me. What insight have I taken from their lives and implemented in mine?

Learning about the 4 Noble Women in Islamic history is often taught as a sort of a trivia question. Perhaps you have even been to an event or sat in on a Sunday school class and the question was asked "Who are the 4 most righteous Women in Islam?"

An eager hand may go up and shout out the answers in a robotic rhythm. "Mary, Khadijah Fatimah, and Asiyah." The teacher may nod in approval and move onto the next question.

As women of faith living thousands of years after the time of our righteous predecessors. We can easily count these as tales of old. Instead we must extract precious gems from the Quran and Sunnah to implement in our own lives. The bravery, devotion and determination they exemplified is beyond inspirational. How did they live an excellent life loved by Allah swt, and how can we do the same.

While I have taken wisdom from each of the women, I chose to write about our beloved Maryam (AS). We know that Maryam (AS) was the mother of Prophet Isa (Jesus, AS) and her life is known to people outside of the Islamic tradition solely as it relates to him.

I chose to focus on a few of the numerous divine lessons surrounding her life before Isa/ Jesus (AS) Here are a few that have inspired me that I desired to share.

Maryam (AS) was the child of Imran (Joachim) and Hannah (Saint Anne). Her father passed before she was born. She was born into a noble family.

Indeed, Allah chose Adam and Noah and the family of Abraham and the family of 'Imran over the worlds

Quran 3:33

74

Her mother was an older woman and desired a child. Praying to Allah (SWT) to bless her to be a mother. When her dua was answered she vowed to devote her offspring in the service of God.

The moments that stood out for me is that it is important to make dua for things that we desire even if we think it is impossible for them to happen. Secondly Hannah was not a prophet and her " miraculous " dua was still answered. We often make the mistake and think we are not worthy enough to ask for things we desire. As a result we don't ask at all or think small. Allah has told us that he answers that one who calls on him. Allah is the creator of the heavens and the earth.

She was elderly, and still made dua for the desires she had. It is important to look at this for ourselves. If we assume to be past our "prime" we should still have faith and make dua to Allah the giver of sustenance. We too often put a timeline on the things we ask for instead of trusting in God's plan to provide for us. My lesson? Keep making dua.

As part of her gratitude she made a vow to devote what was in her womb to the service of God. Hannah was a recently widowed woman, elderly, and with child. Yet she still was thankful and wanted to activate her gratitude by giving her child to be a servant in the Masjid (Temple)

How often do we make dua and Allah answers it for us and we begin to lament over the things that are " going wrong " in our lives. Certainly if Hannah, a newly widowed expectant mother can activate her gratitude, we can too in our times of distress.

(Remember) when the wife of 'Imran said: "O my Lord! I have vowed to You what (the child that) is in my womb to be dedicated for Your services (free from all worldly work; to serve Your Place of worship), so accept this, from me. Verily, You are the All-Hearer, the All-Knowing." Surah Imran :35

It was customary for only men to serve in the Jewish temples. However news spread in the community of a blessed child and the need for her to have a caretaker. While many men competed for the honor to be Maryam's guardian it was Prophet Zakariyyah (AS) the father of Prophet Yahya

(John the Baptist) who Allah chose to care for her. He was a carpenter and built for her a secluded place in the Masjid (Temple) to preserve her modesty.

The lessons I take from this is that we plan but Allah is the best of planners. There were many people who thought they should have the honor to care for Maryam but Allah saw that none of them were worthy and Prophet Zakariyyah was chosen. How often do we work for something and then Allah directs us to something better. Allah's plan is better and surely he chooses what is best for us.

My final commentary of the life of Maryam (RA) is when Zakariyyah (AS) would visit Mary in the Masjid (Temple) and see that she had fruit and food out of season, in her chambers.

Right graciously did her Lord accept her: He made her grow in purity and beauty: To the care of

Zakariya was she assigned. Every time that he entered (Her) chamber to see her, He found her supplied with sustenance. He said: "O Mary! Whence (comes) this to you?" She said: "From Allah: for Allah Provides sustenance to whom He pleases without measure."

There did Zakariya pray to his Lord, saying: "O my Lord! Grant unto me from Thee a progeny that is pure: for Thou art He that heareth prayer. Surah Imran

Subhanallah, here we see Maryam advising Prophet Zakariyyah (AS) saying that Allah provides sustenance to whom he pleases without measure, and he then makes dua for what he desires. We know that all provision comes from Allah (swt) and his blessings to those around us will not diminish what he can also do for us.

How profound is this ayat? How often do we see the worldly blessings of others and we get discouraged, thinking that somehow one person's blessing diminishes ours. We should instead be encouraged and turn to Allah.

May a few of my reflections on the life of Maryam (AS) be a blessing for you and for me.

My dua for myself and for us is that we slowly digest the ayat of the Quran and see the beauty in each of the stories. I pray if I have made any error in my writing that Allah forgives me as it was not my intention.

Ameen

Asiyah (RA)

Asiyah, peace be upon her, is one of the four greatest women to ever live. She is most known not by name in the Quran and the Bible as the wife of Pharaoh, Queen of Egypt. She was beautiful, wealthy, very generous and humble. She is the reason prophet Musa, (AS) aka Moses was saved from being murdered when he was an infant by order of Pharaoh. From a faith perspective she is a woman in history who the Quran offers as the spiritual ideal we as women today can still emulate. She is the feminine example of this sublimated belief .... a belief born at the heart and hand of all disbelief Pharoah. Asiyah spoke up and out against her husband that none was worthy of worship except God, despite his seemingly God-like power over the land and the people at that time. Her entire life she sacrificed and fought against her own oppression and that of her people. Teaching people to have dignity, respect and honor with their actions and to have certainty in their belief of their creator, to think well of Him even in the most destitute of times.

The Definition of Feminine Success

Perhaps in Asiyah's everyday dealings she did not know it but she gave us the blueprint on how to think long term with our prayers even while living through this life. She showed us through how she used her powerful position as the wife of Pharaoh for the advancement of God's agenda. Her most notable contribution is through her dua, supplication to God that we can use today and is found in the Quran in Surah Tahrim.

And Allah presents an example of those who believed: the wife of Pharaoh, when she said, "My Lord, build for me near You a house in Paradise and save me from Pharaoh and his deeds and save me from the wrongdoing people."

Quran 66:11

I was introduced to this ayah during a conference by one of the most respected female speakers and teachers of our time Iaesha Prime, she spoke so passionately about Asiyah (RA) that it not only brought me to tears but I wanted to get to know this woman that had studied the life of Asiyah and was able to articulate and convey the sentiment and allow us to not only experience Asiyah's agony during the last moments of her life but also her strength.

Ieasha Prime is the Co-Founder and Executive Director of Barakah, Inc. She has spent her life as an educator, artist, activist and entrepreneur committed to the goal of empowering Muslim women to rise above their challenges to maximize their full potential of being female servants of Allah and vicegerents on this earth.

I believe she exemplifies many of the characteristics of our beloved Asiyah. When you are in her presence you feel and experience the love of God when she speaks and even when she is not speaking. I am always renewed, uplifted and feel whole when I leave one of her Halaqahs or talks.

Please read and do your best to incorporate this beautiful dua into your prayer regimen:

My Lord, build for me near You a house in Paradise and save me from Pharaoh and his deeds and save me from the wrongdoing people."

– Dua of Asiyah found in Surah At Tahrim

She makes this dua, supplication while she is being tortured by Pharaoh, her husband because she believes in Allah (God). It's so beautiful because she says indaka "near You" before she says baytan "a house". Meaning she placed being near Allah above everything else. The order and priority of her dua was to be near Allah, as if being in a home in Paradise, Jannah wouldn't be as meaningful to her if she was not able to be near Allah.

Allah bless these two women and us the best in this life and the next Ameen.

What do we learn from this dua from a business perspective? This perhaps is the greatest business transaction of all time. As the wife of Pharaoh, Asiyah could have had everything her heart desired of this world but instead she traded it all for that which was right and just in this world; Which meant poverty and ostracization for that of the hereafter with that powerful prayer and instead wanted to be near her Lord without concern for even in paradise having a home. So powerful, God could have brought forth this dua and prayer from a man or a prophet but instead he chose a woman who was being oppressed. In this world she was diminished but in the hereafter she will be elevated.

In what ways can we use the life of this world to plan long term like Asiyah? What impact does what we do each day have on our future in this life and the next?

Thinking long term, helps us to see the bigger picture, become more intentional about our decisions and help us to think and live bigger.

Possibly take greater risks more often with regards to how we stretch and push ourselves to achieve more of the things we want in this life. Asiyah knew there was a possibility that she would be killed so as a believer she kept death at the forefront of her mind, this ensured she always acted with a sense of urgency in her actions. Let me know if the story of Asiyah or Iaesha resonated with you.

What I learned from Asiyah (AS): The people around us (in her case Pharoah) may have influence over us if we are not strong in our own faith, beliefs and convictions, which is why we should choose who we allow in our lives carefully but they do not define us. We each are responsible for our individual relationships with God, we may not be able to change our circumstances immediately but we are responsible for how we comport ourselves, how we react in every situation.

Hajar RA

Be Women of Yaqeen (Unwavering Certainty)

If you have ever heard me speak at a conference, on LIVE or other chat forum you have heard me speak of this Great woman Hajar (RA, She is known as Hagar in the Bible.)

Her story has had the most profound effect on me with regards to both my faith and business. Through her story we learn to "Keep moving searching for the blessing(s)."

If you're unfamiliar with her story Hajar (RA) was the wife of Prophet Ibrahim (AS) and mother of Prophet Ismail (AS) who was chosen by God to be remembered for All time for her faith and complete Trust in God (Tawakkul) and not because of who's wife or mother she was. It's important for us to see the significance of that. Part of Hajar's legacy begins, when she was left in the desert with her young child who was still being breastfed so it was important for her to eat and hydrate. Allah instructed Ismail to lead his family to the desert and leave them there. In his dutifulness and obedience to God he does what he's commanded. Hajar asks him if God instructed him to leave them in the desert, when he answers in the affirmative Hajar accepts her current situation as a test by saying *"If Allah has asked you to leave us here, then He will not abandon us."*

Allah (swt) says: "Whoever puts his trust in Allah; He will be enough for him."

Quran 65:3

One day, Rasoolullah (SAW) noticed a Bedouin leaving his camel without tying it. He asked the Bedouin: "Why don't you tie down your camel?" The Bedouin answered: "I put my trust in Allah." The Prophet (SAW) then said: "Tie your camel first, then put your trust in Allah."

(At-Tirmidhi)

How many of us today would follow our husband into a desert and trust his leadership? I'm guilty as soon as he turned down the road towards the desert I would have had an opinion and a laundry list of questions. From her story however we receive God's wisdom in the situation. Hajar could have prayed to God and waited for him to remove this affliction, but in her understanding of faith she knew that she should trust in her lord but tie her camel. In other words trust in God but there is a responsibility on your part to do something and so she began running between two mountains now known as Safa and Marwah looking for signs of people, food or water.

We know that the story ends well for her son Ismail grows up to become a great prophet, as Hajar was running back and forth between these two mountains the Angel Gabriel appears in the form of a man and strikes the ground with his heel and water springs forth from the place where his heel struck the ground. There was so much water gushing out of the ground that Hajar cried out Stop, Stop (Zam, Zam) in arabic, she then had the presence of mind to contain the water using sand and stone.

Due to her faith and series of actions we benefit from the well of ZamZam until today. The Safa Mountain, located inside Masjid al-Haram, is the point from which pilgrims begin their Sa'ee to imitate the actions of Hajar (AS).

Allah mentions the mountains of Safa and Marwah in the Quran:

"Verily, Safa and Marwah are among the landmarks (distinctive signs) (Deen) of Allah."

Quran 2:158

Each of us has an individual and distinctive relationship with God and we have been given gifts to use in our time here, much like Hajar in her time. There will come a time when we will need to activate this part of ourselves. It's important to create a firm foundation in knowledge and faith and cultivate it so when the opportunity arises we will be ready.

Khadijah RA

Khadijah (RA) was born in Makkah in the year 556 CE to Fatimah bint Zaid and Khuwaylid bin Asad. Her father was a leader among the Quraish and a prosperous business man who died while fighting in the battle of Fujjar. She was married twice before her marriage to the Prophet Muhammad (SAW) and was known for her astuteness and Business Acumen. Through her business she was introduced to the Prophet Muhammad (SAW) when she was 40 and he was 25. She employed him to handle her business dealings because of his honesty and integrity. Later she asked for his hand in marriage. Yes you read that right!!! She has the distinction of being known as the Mother of the Believers, was the first woman to embrace Islam, the first wife of the Prophet Muhammad (SAW) and his only wife for 25 years.

From an Islamic perspective, Khadijah (RA) was notably the very definition of a Muslim woman who pursued and excelled in every one of her roles, as a wife, mother and businesswoman. Her success stems from living out every role in total submission to Allah ﷻ, she recognized her true value was not in any material success, but in dedication to her faith. Utilizing every resource and avenue in her life as a means to serve her Creator.

Through her example we learn how to balance life, work, relationships and more so that we can realize our true feminine potential and live a fulfilled life while working towards the Akhirah (Next Life).

One of the most beautiful stories of Khadijah (RA) was the loyalty, serenity, kindness and care she showed her husband as he was ascending to prophethood. Prophet Muhammad would retire for one month, once a year to the Cave of Hira and dedicate himself to prayer and meditation. This sounds like some of our present day vacations doesn't it? While in the cave one day he felt the presence of another being who held him in his arms in a tight embrace. The being loosened his hold and asked the Prophet (SAW) to "Read", as we know the Prophet (SAW) was illiterate, so the being repeatedly completed the same act and command over and over. Then finally he read these Ayat, which are the first revelation of the Quran from Surah Iqra:

"Read in the name of your Lord Who has created (all that exists). He has created man from a clot. Read! And your lord is the Most Generous. Who has taught (the writings) by the pen. He has taught man that which he knew not."

Quran 96: 1-5

The being then disappeared. We know from the Seerah, study of the life of the Prophet (SAW) that this first meeting was an overwhelming experience and when he returned home he asked his wife Khadijah (RA) to cover him with a sheet or blanket. From this story we learn that in our role as spouses we are indeed a covering for one another and as she consoled him he received peace and she assured him that Allah (God) would cover and protect him from harm. What kept her grounded in these moments was her unwavering faith. When she passed away he noticeably felt her loss for the rest of his life despite going on to marry other wives. How many of us would show this much care amidst the chaos of our many roles and responsibilities vying for our attention on a daily basis?

Activate Female Scholarship

From this story of Khadijah (RA), the Prophet (SAW) and these 5 ayah of the quran we see the importance of seeking knowledge for all people of faith. It is particularly important for women today because without seeking it for ourselves we follow behind others blindly. The attempted removal of outward presentation of Female Scholarship keeps women stagnant, not only is seeking knowledge important for us with regards to learning our faith but also being learned in worldly matters so we move the society forward through our own input and also that of our children.

The first and oldest University was not only founded by a woman but also a Muslim Woman, Fatima bint Muhammad Al-Fihriya Al-Qurashiya founded the world's first university in 895 CE in Fez, which is now in Morocco. Yes Sis! Pick up your jaw, the first time I learned this fact I was like, "Ok Sis mashallah!" Stop letting people tell you who you are, diminish you by putting you in a box. These stories of women who had less than what we have today at their disposal did so much in a short amount of time. She is more usually known simply as Fatima al-Fihri and when she and her sister inherited their father's wealth she used her share to found The University of Al Qarawiynn.

The university started as a large mosque and later grew into a place of education. The Madrasa (Islamic School) Al-Fihri founded is still in operation today as the University of Al Quaraouiyine. It is the oldest continually operating educational institution in the world and was the first institution to award degrees according to different levels of study, in Islamic studies, mathematics, grammar, and medicine.

The University of Al Quaraouiyine became a state university in 1963 and now awards degrees in Islamic, religious and legal sciences with an emphasis on classical Arabic grammar and linguistics and law.

Why is this story of Fatima so essential to our learning and development? Muslims believe that the first verses revealed to Prophet Muhammed (SAW) were the first five verses in Surah Al-Alaq ("The Clot"), which orders people to seek knowledge.

Seeking knowledge is thus obligatory for every Muslim, male and female.

"It is the duty of every Muslim man and woman to seek knowledge," the prophet is quoted as saying.

The Quran also encourages women to work and earn money by entitling them to fair pay.

"...And their Lord responded to them, 'Never will I allow to be lost the work of [any] worker among you, whether male or female; you are of one another'."

Quran 3:195

Knowledge is power but the application of knowledge is powerful, what will you do with this new knowledge? I pray you activate it and bless us with your unique contribution. Ameen

Nusaybah RA

Like Khadijah (RA) many of the Sahabiyat ran businesses and have other notable contributions. There was no sphere of activity Social or Cultural that was not influenced and assisted by their presence. Nusaybah's (RA) life is the blueprint from which we learn about the value and importance of Growth and Development of one's faith and how that positively impacts every area of life. Nusaybah aka Umm Amarah was a woman of the Ansar (Helpers) from the Banu Najjar tribe; She is renowned for being a Warrior and her exploits in the battlefield while protecting the Prophet Muhammad (SAW), she was also very learned in the Quran and Hadith. She achieved all of this while being a faithful and loyal wife and mother. She was devoted to the training of women in accordance with the teaching of Islam. Nusaybah's story most resonates with me and she inspires me to be better in every way.

When I was struggling with my identity as a Muslim woman and also wanting to be a covered muslim woman it was through her story that I found the courage to do so.

From her story we learn that Nusaybah fought in battle protecting the Prophet (SAW) on all sides in a number of battles. The Prophet (SAW) spoke very highly of her and was amazed at her skill, patience and forbearance in and out of battle. What made her fight in battle so empowering for me to wear my hijab is how concerned she was with not showing her Awra even on the battlefield. If my Sister Nusayhbah (RA) could focus and be concerned with covering her Awra while in battle I could surely strive to improve in this area walking down the streets of Brooklyn, NY.

The beauty of women like Nusaybah is that she was learned about her religion and understood the importance of Social Justice both inside and outside of her community. She held a very special place among the Sahabiyat, female companions, once she told the Prophet (SAW) that in the Noble Quran only men were mentioned and women seemed to have no real place or importance. Then the following Ayah was revealed:

Indeed, the Muslim men and Muslim women, the believing men and believing women, the obedient men and obedient women, the truthful men and truthful women, the patient men and patient women, the humble men and humble women, the charitable men and charitable women, the fasting men and fasting women, the men who guard their private parts and the women who do so, and the men who remember Allah often and the women who do so - for them Allah has prepared forgiveness and a great reward.

Quran 33:35

The beauty of this is that it shows the importance for us as women to speak up for ourselves, she showed us how to do it with grace and eloquence. Now everytime you read that ayah (verse) be sure to smile and think of and pray for Nusaybah (RA).

The Future State of Women

The future State of Women of Faith should not be left in the hands of anyone but the women of the society. When we look to the wives of the Prophet (SAW) not only did the prophet seek their opinion but in most cases they offered up their opinion, asked questions and offered solutions for the betterment of the Women, children and society as a whole. It's important to look at the value God gives women as society has diluted and in some cases totally change what God initially intended for us as women. In most cases women of faith are given 2 roles that of mother and being subservient to men. Through the stories of these women we see that while these qualities are honorable, there is so much more we bring to the table. God says in His books No man nor Woman can insert themselves in a place reserved for Allah (God).There is also no need for comparison for Allah has the position and holds and sets the standard. Islam is not a system of hierarchy; Islam and Muslims are created equally as believers, male or female. Each of us has a value and have been given a different set of responsibilities.

The Womb is connected to arsh (the throne) of Allah. What a Profound and distinct honor. The more we look to the women of the past for guidance the clearer the vision for the future and the preservation of what we've been given that stands the test of time becomes.

The pages of the Quran were left with Hafsa,

the Spirit of the Quran was left with Aiesha and

the Tafsir of Quran was left with Umm Salama.

The pages of the Quran were left to Hafsa (RA). She was one of the few women who could read or write at the time of the Prophet (SAW), took the time to memorize the Quran as well and so she was entrusted with the verses of the Quran.

The spirit of the Quran was left with Aiesha (RA).

How many of us will carry on the lit torches from these women?

Why were these important tangible and intangible assets left to the women? We go back to the natural inclination of women being protectors of the culture and truth.

These women teach us that they did not wait for someone else to teach them about their faith, to start businesses, to fight for justice, they understood their own power and stood firm in it while still operating in and honoring their natural Fitrah or inclination.

When you feel positive more positive things happen to and for you; You begin to see things in your life differently; Even things that are seemingly bad at first glance turn into something good

Pray and Grow Rich Formula: The Women

Chapter Reflection and Exercise

If you are currently struggling with your identity as a woman and the importance and value of your role as a woman of faith I invite your to read the book "Great Women of Islam Who were iven the good news of Paradise" by Mahmood Ahmad Ghadanfar. There is at least one woman that you will be able to relate to and you will find bits and pieces of your own characteristics in these women.

What Are the Lessons we learn from The Great Women of Islam?

How Can We Apply these lessons to our life today?

Which Woman of faith most resonates with you?

What attributes would you like to develop within yourself and why?

How can you begin to work on developing them?

4

The Cure

What We Need to Forge Ahead

Our Spiritual and Financial Freedom are dependent on our healing. Are you holding on to old energy? If you are it could be holding you back from moving forward. We need to face whatever is holding us back if we want to be free in this life, let go of someone else's expectation of us. Being content with God having the first and last word. Stay Close to Allah (God) and that which brings you closer to Him and distance yourself from that which distances you from Allah. Use the exercise at the end of this chapter to help assess "What's holding you back?"

God Matures you before you move into your next season. An out of body experience is necessary in order to better yourself, God will put you through what's necessary for you to learn in this current season until you understand He is teaching you to be faithful. You have to die to the old you in order for the " New You" to be born, surrender the old you to God so that you can emerge as the new you. You have to want to be better, to be healed in order for it to happen. Transformation is the acknowledgement that where you are is not your desired state. As people of color we have a loyalty problem. We are loyal to a fault, we will cut off our happiness and joy for the happiness and joy of someone else. We are even loyal to the old us and the old way we think to our own detriment. What about what God wants from us? What is with God is the only thing that is true. Pray. Pray for His forgiveness for forgetting Him day in and day out.

One day in true Drama Queen style, as is always the case with me and my relationship with God its always all the way to the left or all the way to the right, Black or White no gray Y'all pray for me ok. I was having an unusually hard week or I was interpreting it that way anyway and I was moved to ask God in prayer to show me the way to have a better understanding of what He wanted from me and also about my relationship with the people around me. I felt like I kept hitting a brick wall with people and my cutoff game was beginning to be too strong. So the best way to answer the Drama Queens dua was to temporarily sever every relationship except the ones with my 2 children, I thank God those 2 relationships are always constant and we can work through anything.

I'm familiar with the way God teaches me and so when the trip to Morocco I was also praying for fell in my lap I knew to pay attention in every part of the process. God's lessons were everywhere. He was teaching long before I even left for the airport that day. I'll tell you more about the trip to Morocco in Chapter 6: Be A Blessing. To Summarize the trip the message was for me to "Get Over Myself" my failures turned accomplishments and achievements were not about me! The visual of me achieving was and is to show other people what's possible with a relationship with God. Trust me if I can do it so can you, my father named me Halimah which means Gentle, Kind and Patient. That "patient" was a set-up and my middle name is Stubborn, peep the sarcasm here I have no middle name but I thank God for His grace to allow me to grow into my name.

It has been in the failing and standing back up and the strong desire to want and be better that I have found the hope and inspiration to keep going and it has been through my most desperate cries for help that God has blessed me with more than I could possibly imagine or pray for.

Get to the root of your problems and issues that hold you back. Be proactive, seek out your own faults and work to correct them. It's better to deal with problems where they start and not where they show up.

See part of this praying and growing richer is not about money and the many accolades that come with success. It's about moving yourself, growing and developing as you move a small group of people. The people you specifically are meant to impact with your unique gifts, talents, failures (yes your failures count too) and experiences perfectly designed and woven to impact that specific group of people whether it's one, dozens, thousands or millions even.

We live in the age of the upgrade. If you are not constantly learning, developing and improving yourself and thinking you're the best where you are, something better is going to come along and make your information, your product etc obsolete. Be Humble and take the feedback you need to receive from people in order to level up. The moves you make now will give you the results you're looking for later. Don't underestimate small needle point moves.

Stop Playing around with your own potential. I don't care what time of year you pick up this book and read it. You have time. You have time to not only start but finish. You just have to believe it and believe in yourself. If you're thinking about it, praying about it then you can bring it into existence. It may not come wrapped in a pretty bow or served up on a silver platter but you will have it nonetheless. Everything I've asked God for he gave me in some form or other. The only thing He required of me was to believe and be obedient no matter what I saw around me, Hajar made this abundantly clear in the desert.

Don't think for a second that I didn't doubt, that there were no tears. Trusting God after just about everyone in your life has let you down in some shape or fashion takes some doing, but it can be done and you will do it. Want to heal from trauma, trust God and work through the hard stuff. Want to have financial freedom? Get uncomfortable, stop worrying about keeping up with the Joneses. The Joneses can't even keep up with themselves. Face the debt, face your fears about money and what people will think. When I first started my business I invested every dollar back into my business. I went a full 18 months not buying any new clothes or shoes. I recycled what was in my closet. If you look back at my pictures you'll see how often I repeated clothes. A good appearance is very important to me but new clothes don't factor into that, as long as they're pressed and clean you can make a great impression.

Be comfortable being a beginner, starting over learning from past mistakes, asking questions, learning the real value of money, your status as a woman and most importantly learning who you are . Your value and importance is not what magazine covers, Media or any Social Media platform will have you believe. Only you can define what's valuable and what success looks like. Whether your goal is a better education, better living conditions, bigger finances etc. only you can assign a tangible and intangible value to it and what achievement or success in this area will do for you.

Know Thyself

A little time alone never hurt anybody! Spend Time alone and get to know who you are again. As a Business Strategist and Coach my work sometimes crosses over into the role of a Therapist for surface issues, I defer my clients to a therapist for deeper issues. When we go through significant transitions in our life it calls us to be hyper focused on our goals, while I love to see it, I caution against going too hard starting a new venture or business without first putting the wheels in motion to heal first. Which is why in my posts and in my Business programs I include a Wellness Component. Without our Mental, Physical and Spiritual health none of these other goals mean a thing. So I recommend journaling to help discover any mental blocks you may be having in different areas. According to Meg Selig of Changepower the building blocks of self, VITALS are key to helping us create or recreate who we are:

- Values
- Interests

- Temperament
- Activities (Bio-Rhythm)
- Life Mission and Goals
- Strengths

Be sure to complete the Chapter Exercise at the end to learn more about yourself.

Once you do the work to get grounded in who you are, keep that strong sense of self in your business and every area of your life despite the accolades so you don't lose yourself. Also don't allow others to come in and tell you what your cause or business is about or even the way you should think. There's a difference between giving advice and then someone telling you how to think and feel. Be unwavering in your foundational beliefs and flexible with new ideas that further that belief.

Perfect example when I worked on the Not Without My Hijab Play, I had people come and tell me the many ways I could change it to make it more palatable and marketable but that came with watering down the message I was trying to convey so I was not going to budge on that. I also wanted the play to be in high end venues so Muslim women could dress up and feel proud walking into and out of the Theatres we used, I was not compromising on that either. What I was flexible on was when people made suggestions about the cast's wardrobe in the first city we played where I allowed the cast to bring in their own clothes. After the suggestions we brought in a muslim stylist who styled the cast and that made all the difference. If it feels right lean into it. If it doesn't have the courage to say "No."

The quick road to invisibility whether you're at work, in your business or in your relationships is quieting your voice, feeling invisible to yourself. Find the tools and strength within to ensure you are seen and heard by the people and in environments that are important to you. Going back to the wives of the Prophet Muhammad (SAW) and the Sahabiyat, they spoke up and ensured their voices were heard so the decisions of their community were reflected back to them. Be the change you want to see in the world, your actions will benefit others and yourself.

Know the expectations of self and work to surround yourself with people that support that ideal be flexible enough to know that some people in your life specifically family may not share the same ideals with regards to living a life of Ihsan (excellence) Be flexible in allowing them to be themselves, but in the same breath you honor their choices you may have to limit your interaction as not to taint your thinking, you attract where and what you are.

I used to believe "No New Friends" was a thing but with growth you realize not everyone will grow at the same pace, if at all. Seek friendships with people who hold the same values and beliefs that you do, again it's ok to have differences of opinion, interests and lifestyles as this can make our relationships fun, interesting and at times challenging but if the core values are aligned the relationship will be sound. Even the people who betray you are apart

Be Abundant

Life is as extraordinary as the duas (supplications) we make. So what keeps us from success? Operating from a place of lack! "When Women Compete we lose, When we Collaborate We Win." Coming from a Finance, Sales and Marketing background it was very competitive and we were taught to be competitive with one another by the way metrics were measured, bonuses calculated etc. and this scarcity mindset that there were only a few jobs in the C suite kept us scrambling for positions and doing whatever it took to be considered for that position.

From a business perspective there's a this or that attitude, mine is better than yours, instead of a "This and That" mindset and both of our platforms, products etc. add value. A woman alone has power; collectively we have impact. In order for us to have forward progress as women, in our prospective industries we have to get rid of this cattiness, shine together and think abundantly. One woman standing in her power does not diminish another woman's power. How did Rihanna put it?

When the sun shines, we'll shine together

Told you I'll be here forever

Said I'll always be your friend

Took an oath, I'ma stick it out 'til the end

Now that it's raining more than ever

Know that we'll still have each other

You can stand under my umbrella

You can stand under my umbrella, ella, ella, eh, eh, eh

2 or 3 years ago I felt like everytime I turned around someone in my circle was copying what I was doing and I almost got caught up in it. Alhamdulillah, a sister shared this hadith and directed me to go back to my intentions, pray and reset my intentions. Through prayer I was able to see that the fact that the women around me were

doing similar things meant that I was in good company, I was amongst women that were moving in the same forward direction. If we want to use this present life our business to fund our akhirah we must build Subhah, companionship with other women who help to tear down walls of discrimination, injustice and division. This Hadith helped me to be at ease and instead of feeling like the women were competing and I had to be at odds with them that I could instead work on collaborating for the good of the people we were both serving with our businesses and message. If you are in this season right now, I pray this is of benefit. Ameen.

What is meant for you, will reach you even if it's between two mountains. What isn't meant for you, won't reach you even if it is between your two lips."

Writing these lines also made me think of my days in Track and Field, my coach always told me to run my race and it didn't make complete sense until just now as I was finishing this thought. Running your own race or Run your race simply means worry about yourself and focus on your own lane. When you look to your right or left to see where your so-called competitor is, it distracts from what you're doing and the progress you've made. Focus on yourself, your goals and what you bring to the table. Only look to someone else to celebrate their achievements. Before you know it you've crossed the finish line and beat your own best time.

Abundance is having everything you need and not necessarily everything you want. "Stop Chasing Wealth and Simply Become Abundant." Our sustenance comes from God and so pray to Him for what you want and then follow the necessary steps to get it. The perfect analogy to what we must do to achieve the wealth we desire is that of the life of birds. In the morning a bird wakes up and has nothing. He does not know where his food is going to come from, will the neighbor throw out bread crumbs today, will it happen upon a worm that's made its way to the surface, the bird doesn't know. The only thing the bird knows is that God promised it its sustenance and based on that unwavering faith it goes out looking for the food it's been promised and every day he comes back satiated.

Balance and Boundaries

Create Balance

Balance and Success are not things you find, they're things you create action by action and day by day. We often throw this word around not knowing what it means but as something we know we need to have so we are not overwhelmed and get to have the experiences we want to have daily. The first step to creating Balance is to define it for yourself. What does balance look like to you? What does the end result look like by achieving balance? Balance is often the result of a series of actions and its existence allows you to achieve your goals.

Redefine success and be unapologetic about it. This means when you look to someone else who may be in your field and their winning in a particular area you are not jealous and coveting what they have because that's their result, a successful result looks like something else for you. If you want to do work that brings you closer to your faith, work towards that and I pray you're successful. If success looks like having a profitable business so you can afford to spend more time with your family, then work towards that and I pray you're successful. If success looks like creating a family owned real estate company so you can earn a living while you spend time with your family while simultaneously creating a legacy, do that and I pray you're successful. Whatever your goals ensure that it pushes you towards the result you want to achieve as a result of putting in all the effort and not away from it.

Determine what your priorities are based on what your new definition of success is, then say "No" to anything that doesn't facilitate the achievement of your goal(s). We fall off balance when we are not aligned with what we want, our values and the commitments we want to make with our time. Time is a huge factor in how we lose our balance, we 100% own how we spend our time. When we aimlessly scroll on Social Media thats time we could be investing in creating or learning, we have control over that and small shifts can help ensure our time on Social Media is more intentional and productive. When we allow others to determine what we should be doing with our time, if you are in business and work from home as many of us are these days. Your family and friends are the first to misunderstand the idea of Working From Home as usually when they see "Mom" or "Wife" or even in our roles as sister and friend there is some request they make of you. This can be a difficult one to overcome especially if you have set the precedent with your family and friends that you'll drop your priorities for theirs. This goes into Boundary Setting we'll talk about that in just a bit.

Knowing and communicating the flow of the demands on your time is the key to balance and you and your loved ones being flexible is important. There are times where work will demand more of your time and time where Home will demand more of your time. The key is constancy and consistency so when one requires more attention the other does not fall to the wayside. Involving your family in as much of the process as possible is helpful because helping out with the business can turn into quality time and plenty of teachable moments. While this is good the balance is ensuring that there are also moments away from the business where they have your undivided attention.

Easier said than done Right? I know! This is where your prayers come in and fill the gaps. Asking God to facilitate all of these things for you. A prayer for righteous children doesn't just leave it to God to make them righteous but to give you the Hikmah (wisdom) to know when there's an opportunity to teach within a regular everyday life situation. A prayer or worship in the form of Dhikr in the middle of the day, one of the 99 names which is my "Go To" Al Fattah (The Opener) which can open up the pathway to the success you seek, open up your mind to ideas and opportunities you couldn't see before. Did you know that the remembrance of God throughout the day helps you to not only stay connected to God but also ensures everything positive you're doing is in turn blessed? You can do this through any of the 99 Names of Allah, you can also recite small duas throughout your day. This may prove to be the way you can ground yourself during the day, developing this habit will make it easier for you to reach for it when everything is spiraling out of control. We can sometimes add to the chaos if internally we are not at rest.

Here are a few that I have found helpful, I pray they are of benefit to you. Ameen.

Al- Fattah - The Opener, The Judge

Al- Wahhab - The Giver of All

Ar- Razzaq - The Provider; The Sustainer;

Al- Aleem - The All Knowing, The Omniscient

Al- Qaabid - The Withholder

Al- Baasit - The Extender

One Dua (prayer) to memorize immediately if it's not already in rotation is the Dua of Afiyah:

Allahumma Inni As' Aluka Al Afiyah

"O Allah, I ask you for Afiyah."

Afiyah is an all encompassing word referring to overall well-being. This can include health, wealth, and safety from anything that may be deemed as harmful. To be saved from any afflictions, you are in Afiyah.

I pray the dua (supplication) and the aforementioned names of Allah can bring about peace and balance to your day as a believer, as you strive and work in this world remember Allah (God) it will keep you grounded and focused on the true importance of our time here in this worldly life.

Speaking of creating balance I was just talking to a client recently about "Wonder Woman Syndrome" as black women and women of color we are taking off the capes and letting that mess go!! Ain't no awards for it and whoever told us that we had to suffer through to prove ourselves got that all the way twisted. I for one am a hard worker but I find I get more done, feel more accomplished when I work smarter and not harder.

There's nothing wrong with asking for help. Hire the help. Asking for help does not make you weak, it makes you smart and resourceful. The greatest Prophet and man of all time (SAW) got help from his wives, community members and more. Despite his relationship with God and all His resources at his disposal he showed us that to cultivate anything meaningful for people you have to include the people in the process. So who do we think we are trying to take everything on ourselves? This way of thinking is not sustainable so part of boundary setting is setting boundaries for yourself. What old ways of thinking are no longer serving you?

Play The Long Game

Always know that you are just one decision away from a totally different life. It may not seem like it at the time but that one decision creates a ripple in your life and puts the wheels in motion to grant you what you've prayed for. What I've learned in the last 7 years in returning to faith is to be specific in my prayers and actions. God is in the business of answering the prayers we make no matter how shallow or deep, small or big. When we don't ask He blesses us anyway, what we should reflect on when we are blessed even when we don't ask is "Where God is trying to shift me." There is a test and a task even in the unforeseen blessing. Start keeping a journal and writing down your goals, write down the last few blessings you received and contemplate over the lesson. Then see how each of those blessings are working in your favor to help you achieve your goals. Everything is working in your favor. With God nothing is wasted.

Be sure to think, believe and pray bigger, what you want is possible for you. Notice this idea of bigger, more radical prayers keeps coming up and it should be partnered with a side of consistent action.

Riddle me this, why do we think we have to become something in order to achieve something. Or that our success is somehow dependent on someone else failing, how about we stop cancelling people and start cancelling elevating at the expense of someone else.

Simply assume the position so to speak, take our own stance and own it, what we want will be attracted to us. What we learn from Hajar (AS) is that assuming the position is oftentimes us in motion. Wanting a thing is not enough. We have to do what is necessary to meet the opportunity without forcing or rushing it. The notion Stay ready so you don't have to get ready is about doing the foundational work in preparation for the grand opportunity we've been waiting for. Are you a seamstress? If you are presented with a really large order that will yield the profits you've been praying for; Are you ready? Is your sewing machine able to handle the volume? Can you handle the volume? Do you have all the supplies you need? What about practicing? Have you been perfecting your craft in preparation?

Part of playing the Long Game is knowing when it's time to strike and when it's time to sit back and learn, prepare, contribute in other ways to the conversations in your industry. Then Like a Cheetah Mother, hiding in the brush eyeing a Gazelle to feed her three cubs, you pounce. Halal Beast Mode Activated.

The More action you take, the more action you want to take as you begin to see more of your prayers manifest, I pray you are inclined to pray more, not only with your mouth but with your actions as well.

Be an active participant in the life you are wanting to create, be present and take hold of it. The same way we created a budget aka financial plan in Chapter 2, Create a Life Plan. At the end of your life what do you want it to look like and then work backwards. When you are present in your life you won't have to look for any opportunities because they are already around you, you just have to be open to them. For those of you who may be downing yourself and saying that your past is just too hard to overcome I want to offer you the encouragement and empowerment that God gifted you in those circumstances to prepare you for the journey ahead. Someone took your same circumstances and bodied it, God wants the same for you.

I have only owned this whole boundary setting thing in the last 2 years after my trip to Morocco I learned to use setting boundaries in a healthier way. Approach every relationship like a business partnership or transaction, take your emotions out of the situation for a moment. What do I need to be doing for forward progress to happen. What is getting in the way of that? Whatever it is, make it less of a priority on the list but it doesn't mean you have to cut it out of your life completely. Don't be afraid to have those heart to heart conversations.

The people that love you will be there with you through this growth period and those who don't understand will leave on their own. Much better than getting mad at someone because you've outgrown them. Whew!

As we forge ahead to the next set of principles for success I want to remind you that you have the power to create wealth, the only way out is through and you should be inspired by the fear of being average or staying the same.

When you operate in your gift you don't have to be at the head of the table; For wherever you sit or stand, the table and the room will shift. The moment you grasp this concept the ugly side of competition dissipates and everyone can relax and be themselves and we can get back to the business of making the world a better place. With regards to success we've been taught to leave our faith at the door and through the stories of the Women we've shared we learn to lead with faith.

Gratitude

We would be remiss in this chapter on the cure for many of the problems we have if we did not talk about gratitude. Gratitude attracts more blessings to you. If we are grateful for the financial resources we have today no matter how big or small, bithnillah Allah (God) will place additional blessings, barakah in what we have.

And [remember] when your Lord proclaimed, 'If you are grateful, I will surely increase you [in favor]; but if you deny, indeed, My punishment is severe.'"

Quran 14:7

No matter how we slice it our Rizq, provisions do not come from us they come from God, he entrusts the distribution and management of it to some people but the blessing itself comes from Allah no matter how much we think we've earned the right to have it. Therefore prayer in asking for and receiving our blessings is required.

Pray and Grow Rich Formula: The Cure

Chapter 4 Reflection and Exercise

In order for us to begin the healing from the past and progress into the women we want to be in this life and the next we must search ourselves and know who we are. If you've ever been on "Stop, Start" mode in your life or business it is because you lack the proper foundation. If you don't give your thoughts, your faith, your business or your money direction you will get little to none of the results you're seeking

Answer the following questions to begin to get to know yourself.

- Values - What are your values?
- Interests- What are your Interests?
- Temperament- Are you a planner? Or Do you go with the flow?
- Activities (Bio-Rhythm)- When are you at your best? Morning? Afternoon? Or Evening?

- Life Mission and Goals- What are the most meaningful events of your life and what have you made your life's mission as a result?
- Strengths- Skills? Abilities? Talents? Gifts? Character Strengths?

5

The Amanas - The Trusts

What is Our Responsibility?

Every New breath that Allah (God) allows us to take is not only a blessing, but a responsibility.

Say Alhamdulillah (All Praises Due to God) for being the only entity created to accept this responsibility.

Indeed, we offered the Trust to the heavens and the earth and the mountains, and they declined to bear it and feared it; but man [undertook to] bear it. Indeed, he was unjust and ignorant.

Quran 33:72

Be grateful because we have been granted an opportunity to do great things with our lives. With this blessing we have a responsibility to Rise Up

Out of the depths of our own situations and be a help and a light to others with the information we have today. Yesterday we were ignorant to the knowledge and information we have today so we couldn't act but once we know a thing we have a responsibility to act. Knowledge is everywhere we break our trust with God when we don't act on or with what we've been given.

If God has given you the idea, inspired you to pray for it then you must believe it to be possible and move toward it. Yes, it's that simple. As women of faith when we understand our responsibility to God we have a greater understanding of ourselves and we can go forth into the world with confidence, life doesn't seem as haphazard. You can liken this to business.

When you have your Business Plan, Vision and Mission together it's easier to execute on the plan, you don't get lost in a day's work, you know exactly which activities will yield which results. If you're in Sales, your sales reflect the effort you have put in, if it was a great month you can look back at the execution and how well you stuck to the foundation of your Business plan, vision and mission. Poor month? How well did you stick to the plan?

This is the Amana, the trust that God has given us with every blessing and in every area of our lives. It took some growing into the idea that EVERYTHING in our lives is an Amana, a trust. That's some heavy weight, a heavy responsibility, with so much stress and anxiety these days to perform at a high level to meet everyone's expectations and standards but our own. How can we now take on the weight of these additional responsibilities? The answer is simple, work to please God and God will make you pleasing in the eyes of the people.

What helped me to get grounded in this area you ask? Prayer and Quran (or your Book of choice). The best tool in business and life is prayer and guidance which you can receive from God's Books, the Bible, the Torah and the Quran. They give me the strength of mind and clarity for me to move forward with confidence. I receive my best ideas and answers to questions just after prayer or while I'm reading an ayah(verse) in the quran.

Being able to see the beauty of this idea of Amana requires us to connect to God and disconnect from the self and our ego. Ever notice the more you lean into and on God the more He blesses you and gives. It's not always in getting exactly what we want that we are blessed with, it is in receiving exactly what we need that we find the greatest blessing.

Why is upholding these trusts so important? It speaks to our integrity and uprightness as people. We are each given a role in life in general and also in the lives of others. Our children are an Amana to us, can we not be trusted as parents to do right by them? Our work and wealth are an Amana, when we show up to work we are expected to do an honest day's work for an honest day's pay, although your boss may not be able to see you if you slack off, you see yourself and ultimately God sees you. Reflecting honestly would you like to deposit a check or receive money you have not rightfully earned?

Remember you get out what you put in, put in dishonesty and that's what you'll receive. Money slipping through your fingers? Look at how it was earned. When things are not going well in your life, look to your prayer which is your connection to God, if it's shifty there's your answer, when you fix that connection to God everything in your life will shift inshaallah (God Willing).

In summary our responsibility is to "Choose what is with Allah (God)" The closer we are to Allah the better and easier He will make our dealings in this life and the next.

What Can We Learn from the "Five Before Five?"

Oh how long it took me to get this! To understand the importance of each of the five, it looks good on paper and is easier said than done. For all my Millennials and Gen Z fam out there take heed to what I'm saying you will be so far ahead of the game if you start out on the road on a firmer foundation than we did.

The Prophet ﷺ advised to:

"Take benefit of five before five: Your youth before your old age, your health before your sickness, your wealth before your poverty, your free time before you are preoccupied, and your life before your death"

(Narrated by Ibn Abbas and reported by Al Hakim)

For the Prophet (SAW) to give us this warning as a directive, we should pay attention.

Youth Before Old Age

What does it mean our youth before old age? I remember when I was young, I was full of ambition, enthusiasm, vibrant energy and my head was full of ideas. If I knew then what I know now I would have been a problem, but life can only truly be understood in reverse.

While I can't go back and change my own story, I can help someone coming up behind me not make the same mistakes by learning through my experiences inshallah. Which is why I love when I encounter the youth in my travels, I stop what I'm doing to ask them questions and leave them with a little wisdom and empowerment. Being partially raised by my grandparents I understand the value of the older generation sharing life stories with the new generation. These invaluable lessons can help change the trajectory of their lives in a more positive direction. God also talks about the value of the youth and how they can employ the aforementioned characteristics in the cause of God and they will be rewarded handsomely inshallah.

The Prophet ﷺ has told us that a young person who grew up with the worship of Allah, will be among the seven who are granted shade by Allah on the day when there is no shade but His.

(Bukhari)

Health Before Sickness

This is the one we tend to take for granted when we're young. We all were so agile. I remember after I gave birth to my first child, a son, how easily my body bounced back, were it not for a few stretch marks you would have never known I was ever pregnant with a child. Also the quality and quantity of food I consumed and never gained a pound. Fast forward 10 years and my pregnancy with my daughter, that all went out the window. Fast forward another 10+ years and the things I could do when I was younger I wouldn't dare attempt today. As I move through to the next phase of my life and motherhood, I think about being healthy for my grandchildren and being around for them to share my stories like my grandparents were for me. I'm so grateful to have grown up with them and spent much of my adult life being able to still learn from them.

The Prophet ﷺ said,

"Whosoever begins the day feeling family security and good health; and possessing provision for his day is as though he possessed the whole world."

(At- Tirmidhi)

Wealth Before Poverty

It wasn't until a couple of years ago that I learned how money could truly work for me from a religious aspect. This one was probably the hardest for me to grasp initially because my upbringing taught me the negative side of giving and receiving with regards to money. To also be content with when I gave my money in charity I wouldn't always see an immediate "worldly" result, that there was a greater reward in the hereafter for my investments. Surely Paradise is worth the small sacrifices in this life, you can always make more money. You may not always have unique opportunities to sow seeds though. This one has had the most impact on me and I think of this in every circumstance. How am I giving back? Don't miss out on this wonderful opportunity to have the scales tip in your favor.

Allah has promised us that He will repay us more than whatever sum of money we spend for His sake:

Who is it that would loan Allah a goodly loan so He may multiply it for him many times over? And it is Allah who withholds and grants abundance, and to Him you will be returned.

(Quran 2:245)

Your Free Time Before Preoccupation

We talked extensively about the Women around the Prophet (SAW) and how they ensured they never wasted a moment of their time. Think about what it was like when you were young and carefree with no responsibilities, you had all the time in the world. As you got older you were given more responsibilities that took up your time, this happens in the blink of an eye. One moment your single, then you're married and next thing you know the children come. The time we have to memorize the Quran, travel, go to college, learn dua, adhkar or many of the other things that we are grateful for learning young so that it's easier when we're older. It is recommended that we not waste time in Islam and that we should stay in the rememberance of Allah and be productive always.

The Prophet (ﷺ) said,

"There are two blessings which many people lose: (They are) Health and free time for doing good."

(Bukhari)

How many of us wonder how people have time to volunteer and do things in the community? The answer is: they make time and they sacrifice some of their idle time for productive activities that will benefit them now and in the future.

Your Life before Death

It's no secret that we will all pass away from this life at some point, while we would all like to live to see old age the truth is that may not be what is written for us. It's important for us to take this one seriously, we are being presented with a grand opportunity to create our own future with the deeds and the seeds we sow now. One of my favorite books and movies is "Their Eyes Were Watching God" . I watched the movie for the first time at a pivotal moment in my transition back to faith and one of the lines Halle Berry playing the main character Janie said, "Get busy living or Get busy dying." This has a double edged meaning for me in that at this time returning to faith I wanted nothing to do with some of the distractions and spoils of this worldly life that had gotten me to the point where I had lost my faith and had no real connection to God. I gave money away like it was going out of style. Reading the five before five I now understand that even with our wealth we have a responsibility to be good stewards of it. That we need money to exist in this world and making it work for us in this life for the akhirah is not only smart but what is expected of us, we must find the balance.

"If you could but see when the criminals are hanging their heads before their Lord, [saying], "Our Lord, we have seen and heard, so return us [to the world]; we will work righteousness. Indeed, we are [now] certain."

(Quran 32:12)

I pray you take advantage of this amazing opportunity...... May Allah bless us with all five, so we can work harder to please Him and use them to the best of our ability! Ameen

If you have somehow missed the relevance or are working towards applying any of these Amanas (trusts) in your life, perhaps this hadith will help to clarify the weight of these five Amana.

"The feet of the son of Adam shall not move from before his Lord on the Day of Judgement, until he is asked about five things one of which is his wealth and how he earned it and spent it upon...

(At-Tirmidhi)

How We can Apply The Trusts To Our Lives Today?

I answer this question with another question. How can we utilize everything God has entrusted us to benefit our Dunya and Akhirah?

Sis, we must realize that everything we've been entrusted with requires us to live the fullness of our lives and everything God has for us. Do not be afraid of anyone or anything in this world, their lives are orchestrated by The One, The Master of all creation. Be confident and know that nothing can befall you that Allah (God) doesn't know about. This knowledge should give you the conviction you need to go forth into the world with your talents and your gifts. If you are reading this book, this is your season. The time is NOW to act, even if your acts are small at first.

Many of us have some sort of fitness tracker these days (Corona had us stuck in the house and that fridge door opened a few times too many, maybe it was just me) Apple Watch, Fitbit etc. Do you ever watch the counter when you're walking? Sidebar, I know I do especially on the days when I don't feel like working out, "If I can just make 1000 steps, I'll be happy." Don't judge me, judge yourselves. Anywho back to the point...when you first start out one step becomes two, two steps become four and so on and so on. Before you know it your 3+ mile walk or run is in the books and you've finished. Initially you didn't think it could be done and you were ready to turn back and head home, but as you moved forward you developed a rhythm and you were able to press forward.

Work to do this in every area of your life. You have a responsibility to be rich, wealthy and abundant with your faith, your family, your finances and of your course your fitness aka overall wellness. What we do in each of these areas will help us to facilitate the results we want in the other areas. The Amanas teach us that everything in our life is connected to another. This makes it easier to apply in my opinion. I want to be healthy so I can be around for my children and grandchildren. I want to be responsible with my wealth so I can make Hajj, travel the world with my children and attend conferences to learn more about my religion and entrepreneurship of course.

Want to learn to read the Quran in arabic? Make the decision to and schedule the time to learn. Pull up a youtube video and learn the arabic alphabet, then buy an arabic writing book and learn to write the letters, then hire a Quran teacher or tutor to help you learn proper Tajweed (Rules governing pronunciation during recitation of the Quran in Arabic). Putting these processes into practice will help you to achieve over and over again.

What We Must Know For Sure

Being a person of faith doesn't mean we can't have worldly pursuits and must save all our dreams and aspirations for the afterlife, while spending our time here suffering. We can use our accomplishments to facilitate the outcome we desire in the next life. I look to athletes like Ibtihaj Muhammad, Mohammed Saleh and so many more who use their fame in this world to speak up about social injustice, to amplify the voices and improve the lives of others. Had they not pursued a "worldly achievement" perhaps they would not have the opportunity to expose the world to the true beauty of Islam nor help the people they have helped. In everything there is Hikmah (wisdom) and Khair (goodness).

"And in the heaven (subatomic) is your provision and whatever you are promised" [Qur'an 51:22]

Know who you are without all the material possessions, accolades and titles. Build from and with that, know whatever stems from the true honest efforts are a bonus. Know you are and have something special.

"You don't have to be great to start, but you have to start to be great."

Zig Ziglar

Know that Late Bloomers still bloom. Have you watched the movie Black Panther, 2018? One of my favorite little known facts is about Dorothy Steel who plays the Merchant Tribe Elder in the movie. She started her acting career at age 88 and has gone on to do other projects after Black Panther. Proving that it's never too late to start and how important it is to use up every gift you've been given in this life.

Ever have an idea come to you that you don't act on immediately and then you see someone else do it and have great success and you want to kick yourself for not doing it? Yes it's like that. Every idea comes from God and He charges us with them, for us to bring them forth into the world, we must act with a sense of urgency to fulfill them. The

Prophet Muhammad (SAW) although he was fearful of his ascension to Prophethood he understood the honor that was being bestowed upon him and he rose to the occasion despite not being "qualified" in his own eyes. How could he possibly spread the message of the quran when he did not know how to read. A true example is "God does not call the qualified, He qualifies the called."

I pray you're starting to feel encouraged and empowered, there is nothing you can't do if you put your mind to it.

There is a hadith (A collection of traditions containing sayings of the Prophet Muhammad (SAW), with accounts of his daily practice (the Sunnah, the major source of guidance for Muslims apart from the Quran) that encourages us even when the final hour has come to plant the seed in our hands both figuratively and literally. We never know what will come of the seeds we plant with the work and contributions we make in this life.

Anas ibn Malik reported: The Messenger of Allah, peace and blessings be upon him, said, "If the Resurrection were established upon one of you while he has in his hand a sapling, then let him plant it."

Source: Musnad Aḥmad 12491

Know this for sure, God's agenda on this earth must be fulfilled. If we don't act on what we've been given then God will employ or charge someone else with the act of doing it.

God gave us intellect and therefore free will with which to think and act with the hope that we would always choose that which is with Him. May your actions always match your ambition both in this life and the next. May you always be willing to sacrifice your comfort not only for your own development and benefit but also for others.

Know this for sure.

Time itself is neutral; it can be used either destructively or constructively. More and more I feel that the people of ill will have used time much more effectively than have the people of good will. We will have to repent in this generation not merely for the hateful words and actions of the bad people but for the appalling silence of the good people. Human progress never rolls in on wheels of inevitability; it comes through the tireless efforts of men willing to work to be co-workers with God, and without this hard work, time itself becomes an ally of the forces of social stagnation. We must use time creatively, in the knowledge that the time is always ripe to do right.

-Martin Luther King Jr., Why We Can't Wait

I pray you never look back and regret having wasted time.

One of the biggest errors we make is always thinking we have time or we'll have more time to do something. Time itself is an Amanah, we must use it well. When we look back at the Women in Chapter 3, they made great use of their time because they knew their time here was limited. They didn't procrastinate when an idea came they acted on it, when an opportunity came they acted on it. They understood the finiteness of death, while we know this life is not the end and we move on to the next phase of life after death, what we do here in this worldly life directly impacts our destination and outcome in the next life. How are we preparing for that while still being present in this world.

There's no time like the present to accomplish everything we seek to accomplish.

Pray and Grow Rich Formula: The Amanas

Chapter 5 Reflection and Exercise

The more I understand that my entire life and everything produced from it is a gift and a trust from God the more I ensure I'm doing the right thing with it. I'm not perfect and the goal is not to be perfect but to be aware of how our actions and decisions affect us in the long term.

What do you feel are the Amanas you've been entrusted with?

What is a goal you would like to accomplish this year?

Will you employ any of your Amanas to accomplish your goals?

Write it out, Say it out loud to yourself, Tell someone else, then create a plan to manifest it. Answer Who, What, Where, Why and How of it

What's One Thing you can do today that will move you further along in your business or faith journey?

6

True Wealth

How to Be A Blessing

Morocco was the trip that provided the healing I never knew I needed. What started out as a business trip ended up being that and so much more. I briefly talked about how this trip came about earlier. I initially wanted to travel to Cordoba, Spain and visit some of the surrounding countries if time permitted. So I prayed to Allah to grant me the opportunity to travel to Spain and possibly Morocco. I was also praying for clarity with a few personal issues and wanted to be connected with more like minded and like hearted people. Mashallah, in December, 2018 I was asked to be a part of a Woman's Retreat in Morocco.

Subhanallah I couldn't believe how swiftly my duas (supplications) were answered.

Fast forward a few months later to the day of the trip, there was so much peace and serenity all around, despite me almost being late getting to the airport it was as if Allah, Al Fattah, The Opener had opened up the pathway for me. I called an Uber to take me to the Airport and he said we'll be there in 20 minutes inshallah don't you worry. Always a blessing when its a muslim cab or uber driver. We talked the whole way to the airport about my book Not Without My Hijab and no matter how difficult the journey, that I should continue to press forward. If he only knew just how hard 2018 had been for me.

To hear those words was so empowering and I let out a sigh of relief and some tears. This trip for me was not only to impart some of my wisdom on the women who attended the retreat but also to gain clarity for myself about the vision for the next phase of my life. From the conversation in the cab ride I promised myself that I would be open, I wanted to see and understand EVERYTHING God was trying to teach me. I met so many people along the way that I was able to leave a little bit of Sparkle with. Some just by my presence as a Black, visibly muslim woman travelling, others with a simple smile and others with conversation and being open to share about Islam and learn from them.

The two hour layover in Lisbon, Portugal gave me the opportunity to soak in the miracle within this experience that I had prayed for. The irony of this is that we pray within our paygrade, we pray for things that are within our reach that with the permission of Allah and a little sweat equity on our part we can achieve. This experience taught me that I was praying too small. The same God that parted the seas for Musa (Moses, AS) could create miracles far out of comprehension for me. I vowed that day that I would pray bigger than I had been praying.

Alhamdullillah I land in Morocco!!!!! There's something about landing in a Muslim country and seeing the sea of hijabs that puts you at ease. You feel less like a stranger and you can put your guard down. There was something that reminded me of three things in my life before I reclaimed faith, how much I changed and grown and that there was still more left for me to do. My passport photo. So when I left the U.S. and even when I landed in Lisbon, Portugal both attendants checked my passport and handed it back to me. When I arrived in Morocco, remember a muslim country is when I got the looks, the women in front of them did not look anything like the woman in the photo.

I was Hijabless in the photo Y'all!!!! It never dawned on me that I hadn't changed my passport photo when I reclaimed faith and began wearing hijab again. I was trying to figure out why the guy kept asking me if I was always Muslim and me answering back in my broken Arabic. The New Yorker in me was like "What's the hold up" but then I remembered my promise. They finally released me from the mini interrogation at the window. It wasn't until I walked away and looked at my photo that it clicked. I share this story to say, pray big and I mean big, but tie that camel along with those prayers, God is ready to answer so make sure you're ready. Be sure to check that passport Sis, photo and expiration date, you never know when a once in a lifetime opportunity will present itself.

Lesson 5,789,001 Morocco taught me, listen, God's lessons were everywhere! As we moved through to the different excursions we had planned we were reminded of how much we had as we were surrounded by people who had considerably less than us. The irony, they were smiling and content. We were the ones who needed attitude adjustments. We were complaining about amenities they have never seen. The trip through the Atlas Mountains to get to the Sahara Desert was the most impactful experience and part of the trip. As we drove up, over and through the mountains I thought of the people who paved the roads along this path and the people who lived here thousands and thousands of years ago. We were barely making it up these steep inclines in a

14 passenger van, I could not fathom walking this by foot, camelback or horseback. Just as quickly as I would have thoughts like this we would see a person walking down the road, Subhanallah. Occasionally we would stop and take pictures and every couple of hours we would stop at rest stops.

We had two guides both named Muhammad who told us all the history of every place we stopped, the further we moved from the major city the more poverty we saw. At every rest stop both Muhammads would get out and enter the local shop and come out with a bag of goodies. They would take whatever was in the bag and then give it to the locals that were sitting outside the shop. There was one pitstop that I didn't see anyone sitting outside. They simply waited and all of a sudden these children appeared out of nowhere. They handed out the contents of each bag and gave them out until the bag was empty. I watched their expression of joy and happiness and then I watched the faces of the children and they mirrored the same joy. The tears flowed.

When they got back in the truck I handed Muhammad some money and I said I want to be apart of the giving on the next stop, Muhammad said "No", I insisted. Through their actions I understood the importance of giving - The one who receives gains but the one who gives gains so much more than the amount they give. This Chapter is dedicated to the two Muhammads who raced like the modern day, Umar and Abu Bakr to be first in giving charity. Mashallah.

May Allah continue to bless and be pleased with them for what I learned and put into action because of them. Ameen

If you are not familiar with the stories of Umar and Abu Bakr (RA) here is a brief hadith:

Umar ibn al-Khattab reported: The Messenger of Allah, peace and blessings be upon him, ordered us to give charity and at the time I had some wealth. I said to myself, "Today I will outdo Abu Bakr, if ever there were a day to outdo him." I went with half of my wealth to the Prophet and he said,

"What have you left for your family?" I said, "The same amount." Then, Abu Bakr came with everything he had. The Prophet said, "O Abu Bakr, what have you left for your family?" Abu Bakr said, "Allah and his messenger." I said, "By Allah, I will never do better than Abu Bakr."

(At-Tirmidhi 3675)

The Importance of Giving

From these 4 men we have a visual of the importance of giving, there are also many hadith and ayah in the Quran that speak to the importance of giving. Women of Faith from the past are also known for their connection to charity some of which will enter paradise because of their "Long Hands" aka generosity in giving.

One such woman was Zainab bint Khuzaymah she was the wife of the Prophet (SAW) and she is known as Umm-ul Masakeen (The Mother of the Poor/Distressed) because she gave in charity to the deserving. From these stories during the Prophet (SAW) time we see that they thought about money as a tool, they used it like a blacksmith or carpenter use a hammer to complete the job or mission put before them.

On this day my sisters and I followed in the footsteps of Zainab (RA) and walked through the passageways in one of the towns we walked through that has an old mosque and museum with

Islamic books some hundreds of years old. We were not allowed to take photos but it was a site to see how clean and preserved every single book was, everything carefully cataloged and arranged against an immaculate white wall backdrop and glass cases. When we walked out of the mini museum there was a Quran school where the children were happily learning Quran. They stopped their class to come out and greet us with Salaams y'all, Subahanallah, Allah was teaching and using everyone and everything.

We walked out of the school and we were met by more passageways that led past houses and small makeshift shops. One of the houses was a home to a mother who I believe had 5 or 6 children and she also made bread. The door to her home/shop was open, the inside was made of clay and wood, everything was the same brownish red clay color inside from the huge stove that sat in the center, to the walls, everything. The mother was outside and the children came out one by one. We each greeted the mother with Salaams, a hug and a kiss on the cheek, I don't think there was a dry eye amongst us. Without saying a word we looked into her eyes and we knew there was hardship. One by one we pulled whatever was in our purses or pockets and handed it to her, it wasn't something we thought about, we were compelled to do it, seeking Allah's pleasure and wanting to help our sister.

I don't know what dua she made but I would like to thank Allah for using us to answer them in some small way. We walked away in silence and never spoke of the scene except to say Subhanallah wa Alhamdulillah.

When you place more value on the lives you touch, the people you help you with your money, that's true wealth and what it means to be "Rich". When you let go of all the stuff you have accumulated it allows you to take inventory of your physical and emotional baggage and deal with it. Distribute the material things that no longer have value and a place in your life. And heal the emotional baggage. I pray this serves as a reminder of our duty to others while we are. When God increases your status, money etc. increase your level of giving.

The Messenger of Allah (SAW) has said: "Every single Muslim must give charity every single day." When asked who would be capable of doing such a thing, he replied, "your removal of an obstacle in the road is a charitable act; your guiding someone is a charitable act; your visit to the sick is a charitable act; your enjoinment of good to others is a charitable act; your forbidding of others from wrongdoing is a charitable act, and your returning the greeting of peace is a charitable act."

Money is a Tool don't make it your Kaaba

Walking away from this scene with the Breadmaker and her family we reached an opening in the narrow passageway between the houses where the sun glared through, I reached for my sunglasses to shield my eyes from the sun. I touched my head and noticed my sunglasses were missing, I immediately turned around to look back and see if I had dropped them in all the commotion. Sure enough I had and one of the Breadmakers sons was running behind us to bring me my $400 pair of Burberry sunglasses, he could have easily kept them and sold them. I learned about the importance of charity, integrity and honor are what strength of faith are all about and then some.

Going back to the story of the "Food Stamps and the Blue Coat" I missed the lesson then but the Breadmaker and her son brought the lesson and the experiences back for me to finally grasp it, the foodstamps and the blue coat were meant to teach me humility and gratitude for what I do have so that when I was blessed with more I knew what to do with it. Instead of moving about in the world to amass as much wealth for myself for my own gain.

The purpose of this trip was to help me to renew my intentions, for all the reclaiming of faith for who and what I was really doing all of this for. Allah, Al-Haadi (The Provider of Guidance) was steering the ship and answering my prayers, guiding my senses and most of all my heart. He was showing me the importance of giving throughout this day and this trip through this village in the heart of Morocco. We often wonder why a situation, relationship etc. turned out bad sometimes when we look at the intention we find that the intention we set out upon wasn't solely good. The Beauty and the Hikmah (wisdom) of Allah swt is that He knows our intentions even when they're not good and because He knows the future He works to help us right ourselves by creating hardship that helps us to refocus.

If I've said it once I'll say it a thousand times, money is a tool we use to attain the things we desire both in this life and the next. When we take the value of money out of our hearts and replace it with the good we can do with it we reap the rewards and benefits and attain "True Wealth."

Manifestation through Movement

Let's chat about "Manifestation through Movement" and how we can use prayer to clear any manifestation blocks we may have, hence "Pray and Grow Rich." A life rooted in lack will only produce more lack. A life rooted in abundance will produce abundance. To make it clear you don't have to have much to lead an abundant life, be grateful for what you do have and squeeze everything out of what you've been given. Ever hear the saying "Make a dollar out of 15 cents?" My mother was my first teacher in this area, she knew how to stretch money. Despite being poor and at times not knowing where our next meal was coming from my mother stretched what we had.

Before the actual Manifestation stage there is a preparation stage. This is the grooming period where God is creating your story and refining your character in preparation for your mission and your purpose. If you look back this is more than likely the part of your life where you experienced the most pain. Look to the Prophets (AS) and the great women (RA) we mentioned earlier, what grave circumstances did God put them through, before they saw the fruits of their labor? Look to your own life for these standout moments and ask yourself what God was trying to show you and the lessons you can extract from those moments and apply to your life. What skills have you developed that you can use in your current work or stage of life?

Like Hajar (RA), get radical with your prayers and get radical with your action (movement). In the desert Hajar could have easily prayed a bold prayer and sat and waited for God to send aid but again she knew she had to do something and so she manifested her prayers through her own movement and everything that was already in motion to assist her revealed itself. We also learned another very important lesson from her and that It's ok to thrive and be happy where we are while working towards more!!! When she was left by her husband, she understood her fate was reliant upon her trust and faith in Allah but also in her belief in herself. She was content with where God had placed her but desired more for her family and herself and pursued it with vigor. There is so much we can take away from Hajar's lesson and test and apply it to our lives today. The symbiotic relationship of her being taken through this dry desert, using the tools God gave her and finding everything she needed, in this case provisions to feed herself and her infant, was already right beneath her feet. Profound.

Giving Shows Strength of Faith

A theme that I pray is coming across throughout this book is that our entire life and existence is centered around prayer. Everything we put forth effort into begins and ends with a prayer. Inshallah (God Willing, I will) when we make the intention, Bismillah (In the name of God) once we commit and (Alhamdulillah All Praise to God) when it manifests. If we believe this to be true we can also say that our actions themselves are also prayers which is why it is so important to be intentional with our actions and how we utilize our time. Get Specific with what you pray for both with your mouth in prayer but also follow it with your action.

When we think about being a blessing to people as a characteristic this chapter is calling us to task to develop it speaks again to this mindset of abundance. What we give in charity out of the kindness of our hearts is not wasted. It's a dua that you are putting out into the world, Allah I'm giving this praying for whatever goodness you see fit to bestow on me. With the prayers that follow we put in our requests, Allah you know my hardships, my wants, my needs my desires. If what I pray for is good for me in this life and the next I pray you bless me with them. Ameen. Bigger prayers people. Ever notice when you have something to offer at the Potluck lunch, something of value to add to a work meeting or something new you've learned and want to share the level of confidence and conviction you have? It works the same when you give in charity, when you are present to give it makes you more confident when it comes time to ask.

Narrated that Ka'b ibn 'Ajrah (RA) said: The Messenger of Allah (SAW) said to me: "Charity extinguishes sin as water extinguishes fire."

At-Tirmidhi 614

It is proven in the story about Ka'b ibn Maalik (RA), when he stayed behind from the campaign to Tabook, that he said: O Messenger of Allah, as part of my repentance, I will give up my wealth as charity to Allaah and His Messenger (SAW). The

Messenger of Allaah (SAW) said: "Keep some of your wealth; that is better for you."

Al-Bukhaari 2758 and Muslim 2769

Ladies you know I'm pro-woman everything but I value the input and contributions of our male counterparts and I could not write a chapter on wealth and the importance of charity for women of faith and not mention Mansa Musa.

Mansa Kanku Musa (RA) lived from 1220-1337, he took power over the Mali empire in 1312. He is known throughout history for his phenomenal wealth, but his contributions reach farther than that and are displayed in the good he did with his wealth.

If Mansa Musa were alive today he would be worth an estimated $400 Billion dollars, richer than anyone in history and for all time. He was not only Black but Muslim. Mashallah, the beauty of that is he used his empire to advance what was important to him, his faith.

It's important for us to look to these stories for inspiration and representation of what is possible. Those who choose to oppress us count on us not knowing God, history and ourselves. Black. Female. Muslim. representation in entrepreneurship is growing at an unprecedented rate. How are we showing up to lend our voice to the conversation? And tell me again why we're scared to show up? We come from a longline of upright and noble people, how will we continue their legacy?

Everyone who Manasa Musa crossed paths with benefitted from his generosity either from a faith or financial perspective and in many cases both. What a rich legacy to leave behind both literally and figuratively, he is remembered for his faith first and foremost with his pilgrimage to Mecca for Hajj, his promotion of scholarship through the many universities and islamic schools he built and endorsement of the Malian culture, he put himself and his kingdom, West Africa's Mali, on the map.

I share his story to denote how important being grounded in faith is so we don't lose ourselves, get caught up and lose our focus on what is truly important, the reason for our creation. To worship God and to be people that lead others to know God as well. Mansa Musa is a man who could have had anything he wanted in this life and he chose to use his time here wisely and facilitate the best life for himself in the Akhirah with his deeds, bithnillah. That took great discipline and courage. What is stopping us from doing the same? The first thing I can imagine someone saying is "Well Mansa Musa inherited an already thriving empire." Do you not worship and serve the same Allah (God) that Mansa Musa prayed to? We're praying small and acting like God's resources run out.

"One who strives to improve his hereafter, Allah will improve for him his worldly life."

Imam Ali (AS)

Wealth in any form is a mindset before its an asset, I chose the title "Pray and Grow Rich " because if you desire more out of this life than what you are currently living you have to believe there is more and that it's possible for you. That prayer works. Faith works. But Faith without works is dead, means nothing. My contribution to this particular conversation and my contribution of service to the world is to help more women of faith create spiritual and financial stability for themselves and their families for generations to come. You can't control someone who is reliant only on God and themselves.

Lead with service to your creator and everything in your life will follow.

How much greater would our significant additions to the world be if we as a community of women and people were independent of the need of people who are not focused on the same agenda as we are? Prophet Muhammad (SAW) took over 20 years to spread Islam but it was all funded by like hearted people who believed in the same values as he did. Any civilization or cause good or bad that was successful in their mission had a multitude of people moving on one accord from the funders to the enforcers. We must create that for ourselves and the causes we champion.

Service is the rent we pay for the privilege of living on this earth.

Shirley Chisolm

As to those who believe and work righteousness, verily We shall not suffer to perish the reward of any who do a (single) righteous deed

Quran 18:30

Pray and Grow Rich Formula: True Wealth

Chapter 6 Reflection and Exercise

It's important to define wealth for ourselves and work to acquire it whether it's from a spiritual, financial or wellness perspective. Complete the exercise below to gain a better understanding of your vision.

How do you define wealth?

What is your purpose and how have you incorporated giving into your Life's purpose? How are you cultivating it?

How has God been preparing you?

How will you use and apply this information?

What is your Charity Plan? In what ways will you give back daily?

What are the new habits you need to adapt to bring your thoughts and dreams into reality?

What keeps you from being consistent? Is your "Why"Strong enough?

How strong is your bounce back muscle when you fail?

7

Walk In Abundance

Evolution and Growth

I've never been a quitter, I don't think I know how to quit or take no for an answer. My Motto "When In Doubt...... Charge Ahead!!" When you look at "The Greats" in history they have one thing in common, they kept moving forward. Greatness happens by doing, consistently.

So what must we do if living our lives out loud and making a significant contribution are on the agenda? Repeat after me "We must Evolve, Grow and Walk in Abundance." How do we make these improvements? We must peel back the layers and face ourselves, assess what we love about ourselves and define and refine ourselves in our areas of opportunity. We must create our own standard like we learned in some of our earlier chapters. Develop and adhere to the understanding and realization that Faith is not separate from every other area of our life. Instead it should be what everything in our life is rooted in. Allah (God) gave us a unique opportunity in 2020 to reconnect to our faith and reset or renew our intentions. We were able to focus more on what was truly important to us and how we could use our money, business, fame and time more effectively and in service of something that benefitted more than just us. In my 43 years on this earth I don't recall a time even remotely close to this pandemic. Isolated countries and moments but never the entire world experiencing devastation and tragedy all at once.

Allah will take you through many hardships to bring you closer to him to purify you and your intentions, to soften you, to teach you. To prepare you for the road ahead. In the Quran much like in real life God shows you the break only to show you the mend; The hard only to in turn and show you the ease. At the heart of everything He is showing you love, love in its many forms both hard and easy. Think of the most loving and caring parent(s) you know they practice loving unconditionally which means even when they're exhibiting tough love they still love you.

This is done to grab our attention, to grow us, to show us the beauty and the opportunity within ourselves and push us to even greater heights. Are we listening when God is speaking to us? I told you this book was a thought for a few years, 2020 pushed me to pull the trigger not only with this book but also in other areas of my life and with other projects. We talked about planting the seed even if it's our last act. If it was my time to leave this earth in 2020, I didn't want my last moments to be filled with regret.

"What can't be measured can't be improved."

-Peter Drucker

How can we tap into these divine notions and connections from source and use them to benefit us in both the dunya and akhirah.

No One is Coming To Save You

"Sis, I'm Sorry." Once the world reopens I want to do a sisters brunch for sure and maybe even a sleepover so we can chat, catch up and I can hug you and tell you "I'm sorry."

I'm sorry for whoever hurt you. I'm sorry for what you've been through. I'm sorry things may not be working out the way you want right now. Yes they were wrong for what they did and you didn't deserve it. You may never get the apology you deserve, or the acknowledgement that they even hurt you but one thing I want you to know is this, Allah (God) loves you and these circumstances while painful are all part of His divine plan for your life. Keep praying for guidance and understanding and forgiveness for yourself and for those who hurt you.

It's a cold hard truth but "No One is Coming to Save You." Not your friends, not your spouse, your children......you are your own rescue. Seek Allah's help from every hardship. Dua (supplication) changes Qadr.

Prophet (SAW): "Seek refuge with Allah from the difficulties of severe calamities, from having a bad end and bad decree."

Al-Bukhari

"For each one are successive [angels] before and behind him who protect him by the decree of Allah. Indeed, Allah will not change the condition of a people until they change what is in themselves. And when Allah intends for a people ill, there is no repelling it. And there is not for them besides Him any patron."

Quran 13:11

You are just one decision away from a totally different life. It starts with the inspiration, a prayer, an action and then more action. Before you know it you're exactly where you want to be. Stop shrinking into places you've outgrown for fear of not fitting in or being left alone. Strive to make the

Sunnah your lifestyle and Allah (God) your lifeline. People see you through their own lens anyway. People will start to see their failures in your winning . You can't soar when you're tethered down. Pruning is necessary, do so with intention. Those who understand your need for growth will stick around, those who don't will remove themselves. Make dua for them and wish them well.

Face Your Fears & Your Truth

What's holding you back from taking the next step? Is it fear? Different types of uncertainty? Are you afraid of your power? I know I was. The moment I decided to change even after reclaiming my faith there was more that I felt I needed to do. The more comfortable in my faith, the more duas I made the bigger my confidence in not only faith became but it transferred over to other areas of my life. I realized I had outgrown my marriage and many of the friendships I was in. I invited them to come along with me because I loved them and they had already been a part of some of life's greatest moments. I wanted to share this new part of my life and journey with them.

This new season was invite only and God did not invite them. I tried to hang on to a couple and even diminished some of my dreams and what felt like this calling on my life temporarily so that they could fit in it but they could see that the pull on me was too much. Some quietly exited my life on their own, some I had to let go and others went fighting the whole way but when the dust settled they were gone.

It was extremely lonely at first until I thought about how God works. When we start bringing our purpose into our passion, miracles start happening.

With our daily submission to The Creator, Al-Khaaliq and The Manifestor, Al-Mubeen we start being tested and given tasks to fulfill in order to earn rewards and to move forward into the position God has carefully chosen for us.

When I started my consultant firm for Women of Faith in business in 2016, my vision was to help a few people with one on one coaching. Never could I have imagined what these last 4 plus years have been. Every dream and worldly pursuit that I worked so hard to try to achieve and most never happened came to sit in my lap. In turning to God, He in turn blessed me. Faith informs every decision I make these days and when I catch myself slipping away I'm grateful to have people to remind me of my purpose. My greatest fears today are earning the displeasure of God and being returned back to my old life. Filled with worldly gain, no connection to God and no fulfillment.

The more you put your trust in God the more He will show you in different ways that you are not in control of your own outcome, you have to pray for what you want, show up and trust God to bless you with it.

Everything happens by His timing and formation. Each of it coming from a Hikmah (wisdom) that is far more complex and surpasses anything we can fathom. Life can only be understood in reverse so lean not on your own understanding. Thank God for every twist and turn that has led you back to being in service to Him.

"And whosoever fears Allah and keeps his duty to Him, He will make a way for him to get out (from every difficulty). And He will provide for him from sources he never could imagine. And whosoever puts his trust in Allah, then He will suffice him.

Verily, Allah will accomplish His purpose. Indeed Allah has set a measure for all things." (Surah At-Talaq 65:2-3)

Walk Into The Life You Desire

Once you face yourself, gain clarity and conviction of what you do want out of this life you will stop at nothing to achieve it. Until you reach this level within yourself there is no one that can help achieve the success you desire. You have to want change more than you want to remain the same. Walking into the life you desire won't happen overnight but with those small needle point moves I always talk about you will see forward progress.

At first the people around you may not know how to take you. Set those boundaries and keep reminding them of what your plan and goals are. They won't take you seriously until you take yourself seriously by continuing to show up. When you remind them you don't have to be harsh. Just be consistent.

One day you'll be living the life you prayed for, have hope in Allah (God) He is as great or small as you think He is. In this hope, also have the belief that what you pray for is in fact possible.

I am as My servant thinks I am. I am with him when he makes mention of Me. If he makes mention of Me to himself, I make mention of him to Myself; and if he makes mention of Me in an assembly, I make mention of him in an assembly better than it. And if he draws near to Me an arm's length, I draw near to him a cubit, and if he draws near to Me a cubit, I draw near to him a fathom. And if he comes to Me walking, I go to him at speed.

-Hadith Qudsi 15

Know Its Your Time

If you are reading this message this is the sign you needed to go forward with your dream. It's your time.

If you are a Female Entrepreneur or an Aspiring one, this is your time.

As you read this line, begin laying the foundation for what it is that you want to see come December 31 of this year and work everyday to do at least ONE THING to move you towards that goal. If your life and your achievements this year were a headline come December 31 what would the headline read?

For my Veteran Entrepreneurs what can you do to scale or up level your business this year? Write it down and also ask yourself "What's holding you back?"

Quick lesson I learned from getting a Quran Teacher this year that you may be able to apply to your business:

I had a strong desire to memorize Surah Hashr (59) with Tajweed. Yes I can read the Quran in Arabic on my own and have been studying the Tafsir of this Surah for some time now....the difference of having a teacher? Accountability and proper guidance with less mistakes. I also had to put my pride and ego aside to hire a Quran teacher. You know the irony of this? I have been studying this surah in hopes of memorizing it for over a year. I hired the Quran teacher and in less than a month I have memorized 5 ayah and been able to read the full surah with tajweed.

You know what the difference is. I hired help and I made a plan to complete the surah and I executed by finding the teacher, pre scheduling the classes and putting the cost in my budget. When we are ready the teacher will appear, literally. The opportunity will appear.... We cannot sit and wait for opportunities to come to us , we have to avail ourselves to them!! We have to set them in motion through our prayer and continue through action.

Whether it's getting an Accountability Partner, Coach, Mentor or in my case Quran Teacher to move ahead you will need to invest in information and people who can help guide you and hold you accountable.

Need help with the right resources for your business or life direction? Be sure to connect with me. I'm here to help.

Our time is now to create the life and the world we want to see for ourselves and family. Our business whether full time or part time can help us do that! May we be successful both in this life and the next.

Ameen

Prune. Grow. Reap the Harvest.

Pray and Grow Rich Formula: Walk In Abundance

Chapter 7 Reflection and Exercise

What is keeping you from Walking in Abundance? From Walking the Talk? Are you allowing yourself to be influenced by what other people are saying is possible for you?

Has God been pushing you to prune some negative thoughts, habits or people from your life?

Why have you not answered Him?

Who and What should you be focusing on in this next season of your life?

8

The 5 Disciplines

When we decide to change in a particular area or form a new habit or other life transition it can seem daunting. When I was coming back to faith almost 6 years ago the more I walked into the decision the more I saw I needed to change in my life. So many changes at once it can seem frightening and at times even impossible. Will I ever reach my goal? This is where we often fall off because we lack the practice in discipline we need to see things through. Want to know how to "Stay the Course" in every area of your life?

Be F.I.R.S.T. Be faithful, intentional, resilient, strategic and timely. Inshallah in this chapter you will learn how to master these 5 disciplines to achieve massive success.

I Never fashioned myself a teacher but the more life teaches me the more I want to share in hopes of making things better for someone else

I remember once having a convo with my then 17 year old son about moving into adulthood and some things to look out for. He told me that I have to let him make his own mistakes. To which I responded in the affirmative but as your Mom don't expect me not to yell "Watch Out" if I see danger ahead for you.

I find I'm that way in coaching and I'd like to think that's what makes me good at what I do.

Throughout this book I have offered up some of my own experiences to help you create a visual perspective from which to learn and develop.

My prayer is that it is of benefit and helps you go to the next level in Faith and Business. Thanking God in advance for what we can accomplish together.

Faith

"Optimism, positivity and faith create the foundation from which success can be built."

-Sharon Lechter

With faith all things are possible, without faith nothing is possible. Faith is of course your religious beliefs and your connection to your creator. There's another side of 'Faith and Belief' as well and that is the belief in one's own abilities. You must believe that if God called you to do something, to be in a place that He will see you through it. He will equip you with what you need to accomplish the tasks or your goals.

Keep this thought in mind as you discipline yourself to think differently about faith and its foundational purpose in your life; When the hour is established none of this will mean anything. Keep that top of mind as you plan, create and manifest and bithnillah you will grow to be rich and successful.

Nothing moves, nothing is made, without the permission of Allah(God). We are reminded that we are surrounded by God's favors in Surah Rahman, which of His favors, blessings will you deny?

Everyday He is engaged in some affair!

Quran 55:29

He said, Of His affairs is that He answers the supplicant, or gives to the one requesting, or removes adversity, or cures the one seeking to be cured.

At Tabari 23:39

God is available to bless you. God believes in you. God created you with what you need to be successful. You must show up for the miracle you've been praying for. When you truly want different for yourself, you'll move differently.

Do you want Rizq (Wealth), Children, to perform Hajj or other major goals? Pray. If you want it bad enough you'll sacrifice what you love and do. In doing you are also continuing the act of prayer.

What has helped me level up over the years even when I was afraid, suffering from impostor syndrome (an ongoing battle btw) etc. was to pray Tahajjud. Tahajjud, also known as the "night prayer", is a voluntary prayer performed by Muslims, followers of Islam. It is not one of the five obligatory prayers required of all Muslims, although the Prophet Muhammad (SAW) was recorded as performing the tahajjud prayer regularly himself and encouraging his companions to do so as well.

We can benefit on so many levels from this Sunnah. The one characteristic I developed was conviction. As sure as my name is Halimah, as sure as there is a God in the heavens I am sure of what to do next. I move with assurance knowing that Allah is guiding me and will show me clear signs of what's next. After praying, I always gain clarity in whatever task I'm currently focused on, from the ideas I receive seemingly out of the blue, to people that are sent to help me on the path. No matter the faith tradition, or the surroundings, lift your hands in prayer to your creator and ask for the blessing that you're needing, He may not bless you in the way that you see fit but He is blessing you all the same. God is in control of every situation, every bend in the road masterfully orchestrated. This will provide us with the hope we need to endure the hardship, the pain, heartache or whatever affliction we must grow through. Remember you always have more than you think you have.

'Ubaydullah ibn Mihsan reported: The Messenger of Allah, peace and blessings be upon him, said, "Whoever among you wakes up secure in his property, healthy in his body, and he has his food for the day, it is as if he were given the entire world."

Source: Sunan al-Tirmidhī 2346

God's presence during hardship is illustrated in the hadith:

"One day I was riding behind the Prophet, (SAW) when he said:

"Young man, I will teach you some words. Be mindful of God, and He will take care of you. Be mindful of Him, and you shall find Him at your side. If you ask, ask of God. If you need help, seek it from God. Know that if the whole world were to gather together in order to help you; they would not be able to help you except if God had written so. And if the whole world were to gather together in order to harm you; they would not harm you except if God had written so. The pens have been lifted, and the pages have dried.' "

(At-Tirmidhi, 2516)

And with Him are the keys of the unseen; none knows them except Him. And He knows what is on the land and in the sea. Not a leaf falls but that He knows it. And no grain is there within the darkness of the earth and nothing wet or dry but that it is in a clear record. Quran 6:59

These verses offer us the peace and serenity for us as women of faith to carry on with our lives secure in the knowledge that God always knows best. We are reassured that God is in charge. When we slow down to reflect on what's happening God slowly reveals the reason we are facing the challenges we are facing.

Even when we don't ask for help God is near, The importance of praying and asking for help is it helps to calm us and possibly allows the lesson to reveal itself quicker. God loves us more than our own mothers and is closer than our own jugular vein, whatever happened was apart of His plan for us and vice versa. Be accepting of it. Don't waste precious time on what has already happened, instead focus on the road ahead and the way you can positively impact where you're going.

Everything glorifies Allah (God) in its own way. Allah states that everything that exists in the heavens and on earth praises, glorifies, reveres and prays to Him.

Whatever is in the heavens and whatever is on the earth glorifies Allah. For He is the Almighty, All-Wise.

Quran 59:1

Intention

Manifestation and Success can be as simple as making a sincere intention to do something. Ever start missing Fajr (Fajr is the dawn prayer and the first prayer of the day for muslims)? After missing it for a period of time you make a sincere dua and intention to begin waking up, the next day God wakes you up on time. Alhamdulillah. That's how manifestation works. Trust what Allah has for you is greater than anything you can want for yourself. What you take into your hands you take into your heart. Be as a stranger a traveller passing through this world helps you not to get too attached to anything. Two years (maybe three) before I reclaimed faith I was heavy into practicing Yoga for my physical and mental health. I met a lot of people who offered tips on how to improve your mental well being and one of the concepts they introduced me to was a Minimalist lifestyle.

At first it was about decluttering my space and getting rid of the excess and only having things in my space that I loved, think Marie Kondo but deeper. I enlisted the help of my baby sister Faiza to help me clean out my closets, drawers and knick knacks I had displayed around the house. I'm not going to lie at first it was hard to let go and then as each item I hadn't used in years went into bags I decided to donate to the Purple Heart I felt like I was doing something worthwhile. I enjoyed this entire process and my house felt lighter after all was said down. The lesson I learned was how to let go of things and not attach my heart to anything new that I bought or came into my life. This made it easier to let things go. Minimalist living is an all inclusive lifestyle – having a minimal, clutter-free environment is a large part of it, but it's so much more than that.

The Minimalist lifestyle includes looking at the way you spend your time, your money, and even the way you think. The intentional use of the resources you do have. Sound familiar? These are religious principles. Be intentional about your spiritual, business and personal development. Be intentional with how and with whom you invest in these areas.

Don't be afraid of the responsibility of walking into your purpose. The power of self discipline is about being intentional about everything that you allow into your life from people, to wealth, how you spend your time and everything in between. Stop waking up on accident and allowing life to happen to you. Grab life by the horns and take control over it. Anything you want that is good you can have. Be open to it and make the time to create it with your actions.

Oh Allah make this life for me (a source) of abundance for every good.

Sahih Muslim

Resilience

In the 4+ years since I started my coaching business I have helped many women become successful in both their business and life. Everything is not all roses here, there have been some women that I was not successful with some due to incompatibility and others just weren't ready. The women who weren't ready all had one thing in common, they were on a "Start, Stop" train. They would go hard and make significant forward progress and then all of a sudden stop showing up. It was usually after a major win. Right when they were about to reach that next level.

When I speak to them months and maybe even years later they tell me, they were afraid that this achievement, this blessing would be the best they were going to achieve and so they stopped. Please do not do this. Keep going. Resilience requires you to maintain your sense of self and identity as you move through adversity. Adversity can also be your own negative thoughts which I'm sure we all can agree are the most difficult to overcome. Resilience is not something you need only in tough times it is also necessary when things are going well. To push through to that next level of yourself. Require a little bit more of yourself as you move forward. Avoid Failure.....Avoid Success.

See past your present moment, transcend space and time. Look back to the lessons from all the Prophets (AS), they operated as if they already had what it was they were seeking. Remember, God is as you think of Him. Believe what you pray for will manifest.

Strategy

Strategize for the things you can't see, let me explain. We can't see Jannah (Paradise) but we all want to go there based on God's description of it. We believe in God for those things we work and toil for in this life following the blueprint He left us via His books to get to Jannah. If we believe these books to be true and paradise is true then we believe what is in between this life and the next life are true. We have the capacity to create with our current actions the life we desire with the time we have left.

What gets in the way? The enemy. The enemy is not after your money or your stuff, he wants things that are far more valuable, your mind, your optimistic attitude, your heart, your faith and your peace. Prayer must be a part of your strategy, it keeps you connected to the one that sends down angels to protect you.

Assess where you are right now. Be honest with yourself. If you are at "Level 1" be there fully.

Embrace everything at that level soak in all the knowledge you can and work to apply everything you learn at that level. Don't' try to skip levels. You'll miss something either the beauty of the climb or something you'll need later that you didn't take the time to learn.

Make a list of your goals and hyper focus on one at a time until it manifests.

Strategize as to which goal you'll tackle first, what will you need to accomplish it?

Then execute! Sis, I say this with all the love in my heart. I don't care how hard or how scared or unprepared you think you are. Pray and ask God to prepare you for the task at hand. We need your contribution. I've been there and I'm still on this journey with you. I wrote this book scared, everything I've done I had a moment of doubt, then I remember the life I previously lived that wasn't guided by God, I was just existing, not in a place where God could consistently use me and I never want to go back there. If this is you darling, recite the Dua of Musa (AS, Prayer of Moses) below:

O my Lord! Open for me my chest (grant me self-confidence, contentment, and boldness); Ease my task for me; And remove the impediment from my speech, so they may understand what I say

Quran 20:25-28

God will bring it forth indeed, God is subtle and acquainted.

Quran 31:16

Once you get the hang of it and start seeing results, Repeat. Make prayer a part of your business strategy, schedule it into your day. Make it your "Go To" when the day is not quite going your way. One of the most peaceful times of the day as you run your business is when you stop for prayer, express gratitude for your blessings and ask for what you need in that moment or for the best outcome from your efforts. Show up, Do and leave the rest to God!!

Hold fast to dreams

For if dreams die

Life is a broken-winged bird

That cannot fly.

Hold fast to dreams

For when dreams go

Life is a barren field

Frozen with snow.

-Langston Hughes

Timeliness

When we hear about successful people we often say "Wow they were in the right place at the right time. No God perfectly orchestrated the events that allowed them to be exactly where they are to receive the blessings. They had a part in it too, they believed and they made the moves to show up. Would you believe me if I told you "The Future is Created in the Now?"

Be Present in the now, working on ideas and actions that will benefit you in the future. How many times do you come across information or an opportunity that seems out of place because you don't need it now or you don't see how it fits in the grand scheme of things. Learn it anyway.

Learn everyday, when opportunities are presented to you, say "Bismillah" and then say "Yes" even if you think you're not qualified. The idea that we think we have time or we will be given another chance at something has us over think and miss out on once in a lifetime opportunities and then we say things like Qadr Allah Masha fa'al. While this may be true, if you've been praying to have a successful business but haven't put in the work to learn, to apply what you already know or to get to know people who are already doing the work, you don't get to say it wasn't in my qadr. We like to use this as a cop out for not pursuing something. Be able to honestly say I made an effort to see this through and it just didn't work out. Qadr Allah Masha fa'al.

Prophet Muhammad (SAW) said "Seek out that which benefits you, seek help only from Allah and never say you can't do it. "If any adversity comes to you, do not say: 'If I had. only acted in such-and-such a way, it would have been.

Instead, say: 'Allah has decreed (it) and what He willed, He has done,' for verily, (the word) (if)opens the way for the work of Satan." – Saheeh Muslim

I see this during Marketing webinars, "I posted one time and I'm not seeing results." Therein lies the problem, you are not rewarded for things you do occasionally, you are rewarded for what you do consistently. Imagine being consistent for 3-6 months praying Tahajjud everyday and then one day you miss, Allah (God) will reward you as if you did it because it was your regular practice. The same is true in the promotion of your business for the same time frame, you will begin to see results from work you put in 3-6 months before.

The Prophet Muhammad (SAW) was asked about the most beloved good deed to Allah, to which he replied "That which is most regular and constant even if it is little in amount.

Sahih Muslim

Take ownership of the part you play in your "Qadr." Part of the understanding of Qadr is that Allah gives us choices and depending on which choice we make we will go down a different road. So if you don't walk down the road of possibility for the thing that you pray for or are dreaming about Allah will lead you down the other predestined path. "Well Sis, everything is prewritten", Allah says Dua changes Qadr and part of dua is making the request, tying your camel and putting your trust in Allah. The tie your camel piece you have ownership over, what action(s) will you take while continuing to take action and trusting Allah will bless you with what's best. Inshallah. Perhaps it will be what you pray for and perhaps something better but you'll never know if you don't pursue it.

Take action on learning even if it feels out of place right now, better to have what may seem like useless information and not need it than need it and not have it. What you do today will create a ripple effect and manifest 3-6 months from now. Create and Act Now!!

Did you ever stop and think that what makes you poor has nothing to do with what's in your bank account? It's what's in and what's not in your mind and heart that make you poor. What you deposit into your mind and your heart is what will make you richer both by what you learn and what you do with what you learn.

Allah told Prophet Muhammad (SAW) to read despite him being illiterate, he read, which illustrated that with the right belief we can do anything. After reading he was instructed to act and live out what he read. We don't realize how blessed we are that Allah gave us choices, the choice to change or the choice to remain the same. The choice to follow on His path towards righteousness or away from it. Which will you choose?

The beauty of seeking knowledge for oneself versus following others is that you can choose the course of your learning. People of all faith traditions I encourage you to read the Quran and the other books of God and seek not only it's wisdom but to live out the lifestyle found within it. Beyond those books develop your library of books that speak to the end result of what you want to know and be in the end. Want to be a lawyer read, a doctor read, an entrepreneur read, a baker read..... Whatever your plight in life...read to be enriched.

Pray and Grow Rich Formula: The 5 Disciplines

Chapter 8 Reflection and Exercise

Using the 5 Disciplines Be F.I.R.S.T. create your plan what is one way you can be:

More Intentional?

Increase in Faith?

What's Your Strategy (order) for accomplishing your goals?

More Resilient?

Timely?

How can you make intentional use of the resources you do have?

9

Be A Rich Wife

Become the Woman You Were Created to Be

God created us to live richly and he has equipped us with the tools to do just that. As we move through life he adds more tools to our arsenal. Imagine for a moment that you are just starting on this road called life knowing what you know now. What would you include in your arsenal to prepare you for the road ahead? I for one would have had a heap more patience with acquiring the things I wanted and thought more like a Chess Player and saw 3-4 moves ahead on decisions I made instead of being so compulsive.

We know we can't go back and change our past but we can change our future, by the decisions we make today. I implore you to use your past circumstances and mistakes as a guide to help you make better decisions for your future. You can chart a new path. In becoming the woman you were created to be there is a period of time you must spend alone to get to know yourself; Whether it's in small chunks 30-60 minutes a day, a retreat or vacation whatever fits your life.

Make the time to get grounded, be careful not to take on what others see as your life path. It is a major set-up for failure and resentment later on down the line. It is natural to ask the people closest to us for advice and while this may help you get started ultimately you must do what your inner voice is telling you to do. People advise us from their perception of life and of us. Only you and God will ever truly know you.

Learn what you truly want and be flexible in how you achieve it. Go back to the "Begin With The End In Mind" exercise in the first half of this book. Whatever you desire to see at the end of your life, align yourself fully with that and be sure to share it with your current or future spouse and family, so they are clear on your goals and dreams. This way there are no surprises down the line when you start your business and the kitchen turns into a bakery, one of the bedrooms becomes a home office etc. Our natural inclination as women and mothers is to put our needs and wants on the back burner. What we learn from the women in Islam discussed in this book, is how much they included their family in what they were doing and how they moved in unison to support each other. What made it particularly easy is that their life goals were aligned with what was pleasing to God. The more we align with God the more He will facilitate the life we desire.

In the game of chess we learn to, invest in and protect the Queen at all costs, she makes moves the king can't. The beauty of that, is God created us that way. No need to go changing the natural balance and order of things. Each one of us has a role to play within the society and our families. Each equally as important as the other. Although

I'm divorced and still on my marriage journey in being honest with myself I have learned many valuable lessons about things I needed to change about myself to have a more enriching relationship with my potential mate.

When you you pray for a rich husband, become a rich wife, the rich husband will come, more importantly you will know him when he comes. Khadijah (RA) knew the Prophet Muhammad (SAW) was for her. Despite not being packaged neatly in a bow, He (SAW) was economically disenfranchised and she was wealthy. He (SAW) was 25 and she was 40. What she saw in him (SAW) however was strength of character, integrity and of course all the makings and signs of a soon to be prophet (strong faith). She didn't for a second doubt that she was not deserving of such a husband because she knew what she brought to the table. Her formula for success? She prayed, continued to evolve and grow herself, when Prophet Muhammad (SAW) presented himself, she did her due diligence to learn about him and then made her intentions known.

We learn from her and many other women of faith in history how to navigate our marital and other relationships with "Sabiduria", wisdom. We learned to master two roles, being the giver and the receiver, being there for the other without keeping score.

A Brilliant Woman Serves from her overflow.

-Lisa Nichols

Until the opportunity for love presents itself, be the "Rookie and the Vet" be open to grow and learn and use the wisdom from past experiences and about yourself to know what is and isn't for you.

Developing patience and belief are of the utmost importance in this area of our personal development. We are making a lifelong commitment here. Who will be the father of our children will impact what they learn, how they learn. How many of us made temporary people permanent by having their child and we regretted it as their values differ from our own? So much is at stake here that it is worth the time to invest in praying and planning in this area.

Change the way you think about faith, the way you think about opportunity, the way you think about entrepreneurship, the way you think about money, the way you think about friendships and other relationships become the person who would attract the results you seek within all of these areas.

When you're poor and of a poor mindset you take whatever you can get this follows you into every relationship and situation. You go from one bad decision to the next trying to right yourself and your circumstances. In between the children keep coming , further dragging you into this seemingly endless cycle.

The best advice I can give from my own experiences is to: Stop being and chasing average because you think that's all you can get.

And those who say, "Our Lord, grant us from among our wives and offspring comfort to our eyes and make us an example for the righteous."

Quran 25:74

Why is This A Goal for You?

Sis, before you have the qualities of being someone's Rich Wife you have to possess those qualities for yourself, before you try to become what someone else wants you to be, be what God has called you to be.

Be who you want to be for yourself and those you've been called to serve and then you'll attract The Who, the what, the how etc. into your life effortlessly.

As the writer of this book I could easily paint myself as this perfect picture, how much I have it all together. That does not benefit me and it does not benefit someone else who may be going through the same experience. So here's a confession: I'm only operating at 60 to70% of my capacity at any given point; it's not intentional, I'm still growing into who God has created me to be. I still have room to grow in many areas but I'm grateful to have a better understanding and awareness of myself. I'm no longer afraid to be unapologetically myself. The people who truly love me are not afraid of me being "Petal Open" and I'm learning to leave spaces where I'm not celebrated, only tolerated. Everyone of us is learning and growing in a different space. It's ok to leave space for people to grow and continue ahead on the journey. Perhaps our paths will cross again somewhere down the line.

Another truth is there's still part of me that can't believe this is my life. I get to live out my life feeling fulfilled and pretty much having full control of my day, free to worship, just be, have fun and make money in the process. Some days are hard and I go to bed tired and exhausted but the days where I feel accomplished and fulfilled are so worth it.

Feminine energy is powerful as women. We need to understand our natural inclination, our Fitrah and rest in our power. There is so much power in the calmness of our nature. Being ourselves speaks volumes. Society would have us believe that we have to become masculine or become something else in order to be successful. When we look at the stories that we shared earlier in this book we see that those women rested in their power, the greatness and fullness of who they were and future generations get to bask in their accomplishments that were produced from them being naturally themselves.

Define What A Rich Wife Is To You

I have talked about the benefit of looking to the future at what you want and making that the goal post. This helps us not to get trapped by the opinion of others. When we create our own life plan and we acknowledge our own goals we take back control of our lives. It is up to us to give birth to our dreams within our lifetime, beginning with the end in mind we set the goal line, when people and opportunities come to us we must remain resolute as not to veer off our life path. In the game of chess the more moves ahead you can foresee increases the likelihood of you being able to anticipate the possible strategy and in turn secure the outcome. Imagine a society where every single person within the society has clear goals, a clear vision for the future and how much more impactful that society would be.

A rich wife understands the power of community and sisterhood. Nothing is accomplished alone. When we look at the wives of the Prophet (SAW) and we look to women in history who accomplished so much within their lifetimes we can look to the right or the left or all around them and we're able to see that they collaborated with other women. I enjoyed the story "Self Made" on Netflix based on the life of Madame CJ Walker this past summer because it showed how she put herself on, hence the title and then she was able to put other women on, my goal in saying this and talking about this is to encourage collaboration over competition with women.

We don't have to know everything. We just have to be clear on our goals and know the right people. Networking with other women is a part of the learning process. Bringing people into our life that we can learn from and teach this teaches us how to reciprocate what we're given. Collaboration is key to our success. It is key for us in becoming that rich wife prior to even coming into marriage. How we treat ourselves and the people around us will be how we will treat our spouses inside of a relationship. A poor mindset will keep us from collaborating. When we develop an abundant mindset and understand that working together with other women, not only benefits us in our individual pursuits but uplifts us collectively. When other women see these types of collaborations it becomes the path for other women to follow.

Become Her For Yourself

Don't go looking for a rich husband, be a rich wife, right there where you're at. Before you head out on that road looking for someone to "complete you", be complete and whole yourself. We don't need anymore relationships where each person is bringing fifty percent of themselves to the table. We need two people coming together willing to put in 100% of themselves into the relationship. Ensure what you require in a spouse you can reciprocate. Want to be able to hold an intelligent conversation? Commit to learning one new thing everyday. Want someone who is well travelled? Be well traveled yourself. What's your passport looking like? Want someone who is wealthy, has assets? Have a wealthy mindset and assets yourself. Be a reflection of what you expect.

As women of faith it's time we teach this approach to our daughters, to the generations coming behind us. Society and Media would have you believe that the prize is the husband when in fact the prize is both people in the relationship, the prize is you living out your life fully, the other person living out their life fully and coming together and sharing a life together.

I come from two minority communities the Black Community and the Muslim Community where these concepts are not taught from a broader lens, we don't look outside our four walls and look to the contribution each individual family makes towards the whole of society. It's time for us to build our own table, bring our own chairs and teach our children, our daughters specifically how to build theirs and build them early so they don't have to ask a stranger for a seat at their table or a person who does not have them in mind with their policies and politics.

What I'm suggesting is bigger than being a wife or husband for ourselves it's about treating marriage as an entity that produces energy and results in work that positively shifts and promotes the welfare of an entire society.

Be Specific and Pray for Your Rich Husband, Rich Family and a Rich Life

Be specific in your prayer. Know the criteria for your rich husband, your rich family and your rich legacy. If you want to attract what you want, decide what that is and then decide that it is possible for you to have that, down to the most finite details. See you can't believe that God is a God of miracles in one area of your life and then turn it off in another area in your life.

At the end of this chapter make sure you take advantage of the exercise on envisioning your spouse, your life with your spouse and how you can become the wife fitting of that spouse before you undertake the process of marriage.

"When Allah wants two hearts to meet, he will move both of them, not just one."

-Unknown

Marriage is an integral part of a person's life and should not be taken lightly. Foster an environment that would produce the results you would like to see. Attain the education both formal and informal that you want to have; Develop your faith to a level that would assist you in such a relationship. If you want to cook certain meals for your future family, perfect them. You want to travel to certain places, make Hajj etc. learn the language, study and write down the places you'd like to go. Come to the conversation with something to offer even if in the beginning it's fully formulated ideas for when the right opportunity presents itself. When you pray for your husband specifically and with intention your strengths as well as your shortcomings won't deter that person.

As seen with the wives of the Prophet (SAW) many of his wives were divorcees, affluent, some slaves etc. these were seen as positive characteristics that didn't reduce their chance of getting married. Today we have attributed these as negative or undesirable when getting married, but for the right person, you are in fact the perfect person for them.

The perfect example are Khadijah (RA) and Prophet Muhammad (SAW) They were both PRIZES. Highly sought after for marriage in their time. Khadijah (RA) bought the character, economic and societal power needed to fund and facilitate the advent of Islam and Muhammad (SAW) bought prophethood and God's promise of Jannah, the perfect compliment and suitable partner one to the other.

Women impure are for men impure, and men impure for women impure, and women of purity are for men of purity, and men of purity are for women of purity: these are not affected by what people say: for them there is forgiveness, and a provision honorable.

Quran 24:26

From this ayah we learn that the more we work on and develop ourselves the more we will become a reflection of the person we want in a spouse or any relationship for that matter. When we don't work on ourselves what comes into our lives kinda sorta looks like what we want. If you are like most women, including me we try to make it fit. As my mother always used to say "You can't fit a square peg into a round hole." It's never going to work.

Prophet Muhammad (SAW) in his "Farewll Pilgrimage (Hajj)He said, "Oh people, you have rights over your wives, and your wives have rights over you. Remember, you must always treat your wives with kindness. Woman is weak and cannot protect her own rights. When you got married, God appointed you the trustees of those rights. You brought your wives to your homes under the Law of God. You must not, therefore, insult the trust which God has placed in your hands."

Prophet Muhammad advised Muslims to marry; he forbade the practice of celibacy. He said, "Marriage is my precept and my practice. Those who do not follow my practice are not of me." He also said, "When a man has married, he has completed one half of his religion."

What is your Kaaba? What does your life revolve around? You can use the exercises from the previous chapters to be able to dig deep and figure this out for yourself. The beauty of this book "Pray and Grow Rich " and this concept is that we can indeed pray and grow rich in every area of our life, faith , family, finances and fitness (our overall wellness). Know that tawakkul is currency, faith is currency, prayer and worship are currency.

It's important for us to see the value in our role models, like Khadijah (RA), the women of the Quran Asiyah(AS) and Maryam(AS). Align yourself with people and values that are like hearted that have the same values and are reaching for the same ultimate goal as you, as women of faith we are reaching for paradise we are reaching for Jannah. Be ok with the fact that the goals we have or the steps that we take are not going to look like that of the people of the rest of society. It's our responsibility to work with other women to create a high society of women with even higher standards.

In all this internal work, you will be tested to see how badly you want what you pray for. Don't let anybody take you out of pocket! Repeatedly go back and check your intentions.

Society has taught us that getting what we want immediately is the prize; it is what our goal in acquiring success should look like. Patience is a weakness, that the only discipline we need to have is in having the right technology and information to get there the fastest. I'm here to tell you it's ok to take the road less travelled, the indirect route to success, we're playing chess, not checkers.

Work on something that will speak for you long after you're gone, that's legacy. Be intentional in your giving. Check God's Blueprint. Which are the deeds that have the potential to earn the most reward? Which are the deeds most beloved to Allah (God). Practice patience and look for the opportunities for growth within every situation.

Be BEAUTIFUL

You are not who others think or say you are,

You are who Allah (God) knows you are,

who He created you to be.

Keep growing into her.

Allow yourself to be refined by your lessons and experiences. Pray for knowledge, discernment and the discipline to become her.

Then Walk into the life you've prayed for, for her. You've put in the work so own it, you deserve to be there.

You have a great responsibility as a woman in society don't let anyone diminish your role, be beautiful from the inside out as God intended. Whether you're a stay at home Mom, a Business or Career woman you give birth to half of society, what an honor and a privilege. In the book Great Women of Islam we mentioned in Chapter 3, I was surprised by how many of the 27 women had been divorced and some divorced a few times over. Today there is so much shame around being divorced and what I learned from these women as a Divorcee myself is that they never compromised their values or their faith. If they were in incompatible relationships they gave it their best and then severed ties. And after divorce they stayed to themselves until a better suitor came along and they were approached or they themselves approached the suitor for marriage.

The Prophet SAW said "A woman is sought in marriage for four reasons; wealth, social status, beauty and deen (piety). So seek the one with deen – may you then be successful." . He has clearly made an emphasis on deen as the one quality that supersedes all other qualities. That is not to say one should not look for a spouse with other attributes like beauty, it just means that deen (religion) should be your main focus.

Bukhari & Muslim

You are your own best thing. There is no other being, created better than you. Do you know that? That of all God's creation you are His most prized. The day you realize and know that, is the day that you will stop being afraid to live full out. The beauty of you living full out is the world benefits and gives other women permission to do the same. Before you pray for the husband, pray for the wife qualities of the woman deserving of that husband. Pray for God to show you ALL the beauty within yourself, the intelligence and the overall value you possess so you don't need to look outside of you for that validation. You can come into a relationship whole instead of broken and in pieces, or coming with half a whole trying to become whole. That's where we go left in relationships FYI, they don't have a chance before they even start.

Part of being beautiful is to surround yourself with people who are lighthearted and beautiful. Beautiful from the inside out. Who you love you for Allah's sake and want the best for you without coveting what you have for themselves. Did you ever stop and think that perhaps someone talks you out of a thing because they secretly coveted it for themselves and seeing you acquire it and achieve it causes them to face areas of themselves where they're deficient or dreams and goals they've given up on? Pray for them. Keep the people who fan your flames, give you constructive feedback when necessary and want the best for you in this life and the next.

One of the greatest lessons that I learned as a woman of faith in business and life is that two or more things can be true at once this helps me to collaborate and share more. If two women are in the same field, the same marriage even, as was the case with Prophet Muhammad (SAW) they're doing the same thing, they don't have to compete. Beauty is in the eyes of the beholder, in this case the eyes of the Prophet (SAW) each of his wives served a purpose and was beloved to the Prophet. Instead of competing against each other they worked together towards a common goal.

Today, you can subscribe to a woman that's doing the same work that another woman is doing or have two mentors that are in the same field but one gives you one thing and the other gives you something else. You don't have to choose one over the other, you can have a relationship with them both. The Sun is not better than the moon, they serve two different purposes. The same goes for our role as women, let's normalize celebrating more than one woman for the work they're doing at the same time without the need for comparison and diminishing one another.

Coincidences are the way God helps himself remain anonymous.

-Cat Stevens a.k.a. Yusuf Islam

Surah 24, Verse 32) \\"And let those who cannot find someone to marry maintain chastity until Allah (SWT) makes them rich through His favours

From everything we've learned throughout this book I know it can be pretty scary to start and to lean all the way into that one thing, to lean in to what we believe as women of faith mostly because our ideas and ways of thinking are part of the minority. Know that there is so much power in that. Our society is controlled by the 1% because they possess economic power. We possess something far greater, prayer and faith. With God we have everything, without Him we have nothing. We can appear powerful in this worldly life and be struggling spiritually. That which is more lasting and true is with God remember that.

Focus on your greatness. Focus on that one thing that you're great at people will gravitate toward you they will gravitate toward your authenticity. Once they're in you can show them what else you have to offer. Know that if you don't Live by your own rules you'll die by someone else's. What grounds you? How willing are you to take hold of your Destiny? In this life we need money and influence to build schools, communities etc. to serve our way of life yet we shy away from or sabotage opportunities to require the resources for us to do so. This is particularly prevalent in poor, black and Muslim communities. How many of us have ownership over ourselves? Property? Or our community?

These ideas may seem complex but they are accessible. Let's normalize excellence as accessible. Excellence is simple and special. Ever really look at the word Extraordinary? When we think of people who do great things we call them Extraordinary. This word pairs together two words "extra" and "ordinary", simple and special. The greatest people in history led simple lives, were true to themselves and accessed that special thing about them and shared it with the world. Accessible Excellence, means reaching for that level of ourselves, learning from the past and bringing those things together to change the narrative and the trajectory of our people.

As women we are not a monolith. We must define ourselves to the world and not let them tell us who we are. We must show up every single day just as we are. Utilize the tools around us , social media, podcast, Youtube they provide us with our own radio and TV channels where we can broadcast our message to the masses 24/7 with no barrier to entry. We can utilize our platforms to take back control of our own narrative as women of faith, as wives, aunties and mothers it is our responsibility to be the backbone of the community and to continue the legacy of our culture, to continue the legacy of our values and our beliefs. You see being a rich wife is not about being a wife at all it is about being a contributor to our society and ensuring that our future generations inherit something far greater than what we ourselves inherited. Something we have created versus inherited, it's about taking back control of our voice, taking back control of what our communities produce and so much more.

Having been a wife twice, my marriage journey has taught me that it's never too late and you're never too far gone to start over to flip the script to change how the story ends.

When you start over this time don't be afraid to start from scratch this time you are starting from experience.

I pray that through this book you understand that the idea of "Pray and Grow Rich" is not just about money. There are a multitude of investments we must make to acquire what we need to accrue the capital, the assets to move our lives forward individually and collectively. It starts with making the time investment to be thoughtful about the life we want to cultivate for ourselves and our children. Learning our faith helps us to learn ourselves, the more we know ourselves the clearer the overall objective of our lives becomes. It's like looking across the plains from your farmhouse door, you can see clear across. Faith allows us to see to the other side plainly even once we let the animals loose on the farm, because we've seen the vision no matter what obstructs the path we can still see it plainly.

When the angel Gabriel (AS) asked the prophet Muhammad (SAW) to read that was about him acquiring knowledge so that he could implement it and teach it to the people. The more they knew themselves and their purpose in life the more upright they were able to stand. People couldn't sway them from the path. How do you flip an investment in Business, ask yourself what am I going to build that will make me five times this investment? That's how we have to look at this life. How can I utilize the gifts I've been given in this world to facilitate my life in the next?

Chapter 9 Reflection and Exercise

Close your eyes envision the life and the relationship that you want to create imagine yourself as we did in the opening of this book as you walk on that beach in your favorite place in the world as you walk down the street and you're holding the hand of the spouse of your dreams what do you want that day to look like what do you want to be surrounded by who do you want to be surrounded by. When you have that perfect picture envisioned and in mind work backwards.

What do you want? What are the hundred plus qualities of your soulmate? What are the hundred plus qualities a husband like that needs in a wife?

Write down pray and work for the characteristics you want your current or future spouse to have become the best version of yourself by becoming the wife to serving of these before marriage for yourself and within work together with your spouse to become better for each other

Ask yourself: Why are you getting married?

Once you have the criteria enlist the help of your family or friends to help you find a suitable spouse. Ensure every person knows what they're role will be.

Follow the proper guidelines of lowering your gaze etc when together with the opposite sex.

The Prophet said: "Whenever a man is alone with a woman the Shaytan makes a third"

At-Tirmidhi

He also advised men: "Not one of you should meet a woman alone unless she is accompanied by a relative within the prohibited degrees"

Bukhari, Muslim

Final Thoughts

Perhaps I should have named this book "Pray and Grow Richer". How many of you started to notice throughout this book that you already had the beginnings, if not the full idea of what you want your life, business or next project etc. to look like? It's because it's innately within you. God knew you and what you were capable of doing long before you got here. He's waiting for you to take hold of it.

Your worth to the world is the value you place on yourself. Want to be an irreplaceable one of a kind gem? Simply be it. Be it by the value you bring to people. Whether it's kindness through your actions, words of wisdom and/or charity in all forms. Aim to enrich the lives of others, leave people and places better than you found them.

Want to be successful in this life and the next? Keep the line of communication open with Allah (SWT) through sincere and consistent prayer.

"O you who believe! Respond to (the call of) Allah and His Messenger when he calls you to that which gives you life."

Qur'an 8:24

"The closest a person is to His Lord is when he is in prostration"

The pens have been lifted and the ink is dry. Pray because Prayer changes the course of our Qadr, predestination. Allah (God) knows all that will occur, without interfering with our free will. Meaning through free will, we can choose one choice and it will rechart our course.

If you are uncomfortable after reading this book you are in the perfect place to start to make a change. Change and doing something you've never done before is not supposed to feel comfortable and easy. If it was everyone would do it and there wouldn't be a need for books like this one.

I pray as you grow you continually choose to Pray and Grow Rich.

"That Allah may forgive thee of thy faults that which is past and that which is to come, and may perfect His favour/Ni'mat unto thee, and may guide thee on a right path".

Quran 48:2

Bonus Chapter:
The 60 Minute Startup

How to Build A Business for Impact and Profit

Mindset

Inshallah I'm going to give you a million dollars worth of information in a few short pages. Alhamdulillah through my Business Coaching firm Be You In HD, LLC I have helped a few dozen female owned businesses build six and seven figure businesses in 2 years or less. This was achieved with consistent daily effort, strategy and weekly assessments of sales and marketing strategies.

You have to have the right mindset from the beginning in order to achieve these results. You don't have to have everything figured out to start. Know where you want to be in the next 5-10 years as a result of your business and who you want to help and you're halfway there. Bring the strong desire to grow to your consultation or on Day 1 of our Boss Hijabi Society/Academy "Build Your Boss Biz in 90 days" 13 week program and we will help you do the rest. We can teach you a new skill but you have to bring the will.

A Woman of Faith in Business aligns her passion with her purpose, while simultaneously serving her Creator and community. She must lay a firm foundation, know herself inside and out to be able to strategically advance her faith, family, finances, and fitness (overall wellness). An essential part of growth through entrepreneurship is not being afraid to fail, execute on the first idea and every idea after that before your brain has a chance to catch up. Don't be afraid to shift or pivot when necessary, take massive steps forward creating freedom, flexibility and a positive impact for your life and others.

5 Quick Steps for Building a Successful Online Business

1. Find Your Niche
2. Ensure its a Viable Idea
3. Conduct Research & Analyze the Market
4. Create and or Source Products
5. Choose E- Commerce platform

Unsure of which business you would like to create?

Ask yourself these questions:

What Do You Dream of Most Often?

What Business Ideas come to you?

Complete this 7 minute exercise:

Take a blank piece of paper

(No lines as not to inhibit the creative process)

Write down the Business Idea you want to explore

What Problems will your Business Solve?

266

Next Write Down the Ideas for Purpose and Products of that Business (Write Down Every Possibility)

Where to Start

Product Selection- Choose the product(s) you want to sell whether product or service based or hybrid business

Target Audience- This is by far the most important step in creating your business; Without knowing who you serve you will not be able to properly serve, sell or market your product or service to them.

1-3 Page Business Plan- Create a quick reference Business Plan that includes your Vision, Mission, Financial and Sales and Marketing Plan.

Create a Timeline- Create a tentative timeline for your business including product production time, launch, Sales platform etc.

Branding- Build your Brand Strategy which includes the look and feel of your brand, brand story, business purpose and more.

Budget- How much money will you need to start your business? Do you need product, supplies and office space etc to start? Create the budget even if you don't have the money. This will provide you with a goal to reach for; a purpose to set your plan in motion.

Business Formation

Use the Small Business Administration (www.sba.gov) to begin to research which type of business you would like to form (Sole Proprietorship, LLC, S-Corp etc.)

What's Next

Be sure to surround yourself with like minded women in business, it is only natural that we share with the people that are closest to us. Don't be surprised if they don't share your entrepreneurial enthusiasm. It in no way means you should trash the entire idea. It means you need to find people that have an appreciation for where you are and where you're going. That can offer you support and sound advice on where you should go next. Whether they're a coach, mentor, accountability partner or entrepreneurial community.

The Boss Hijabi Society I founded in May 2018 as an in person Brunch series expanded in 2020 to include an online community, Boss Hijabi Academy. Co-Created with Amber Von Grat and I to teach you how to align disciplined action with your desired results via webinars, conferences and events.

BHS uses a holistic approach to help like minded women connect spiritually, heal emotionally, lead an active lifestyle and grow financially. You can learn more about us at www.bosshijabisociety.com

Our monthly programs, which includes our 13 week Build Your Boss Business in 90 Days program are designed to take you from feeling unworthy, stressed and incapable, to becoming a confident and successful "Boss Hijabi" both in life and business.

And said, 'Ask forgiveness of your Lord. Indeed, He is ever a Perpetual Forgiver.

He will send [rain from] the sky upon you in [continuing] showers.

And give you increase in wealth and children and provide for you gardens and provide for you rivers.

Quran 71:10-12

Made in the USA
Middletown, DE
02 April 2021